Creative Writing

CREATIVE WRITING

A Handbook for Teaching Young People

Kathleen C. Phillips
and
Barbara Steiner

Illustrated by
Robert B. Phillips

1985
LIBRARIES UNLIMITED, INC.
Littleton, Colorado

LIBRARIES UNLIMITED, INC.
P.O. Box 263
Littleton, Colorado 80160-0263

Library of Congress Cataloging in Publication Data

Phillips, Kathleen C.
    Creative writing.

    Includes index.
    1. Creative writing (Elementary education)--Handbooks,
manuals, etc. I. Steiner, Barbara A. II. Title.
LB1576.P576 1985   372.6'23   84-29679
ISBN 0-87287-488-5

Libraries Unlimited books are bound with Type II nonwoven material that meets
and exceeds National Association of State Textbook Administrators' Type II
nonwoven material specifications Class A through E.

For
Jane Fitz-Randolph
Teacher Summa Cum Laude

Contents

Preface

Creative Writing: A Handbook for Teaching Young People is the book you have asked us for. It is the result of our workshops with both children and teachers. While we use many of these same techniques with high school students and adults, this book is directed most specifically to you teachers of elementary and middle schools. It gives answers to questions you have asked, to problems you have presented, and it has been compiled for your use, in response to your requests. We have not included scholarly research for those who prefer such terms as *sequential analysis* to *And then what happened?* or *rational intent* rather than *Why?* Nor have we included "current techniques in evaluation and holistic scoring" because we do not believe that competitive grading has any place in considering a child's personal, imaginative creations.

This book emphasizes the freedom of creation tempered with the discipline of revision. It presents reasons for encouraging children to write and motivations and techniques for helping them to write. It shows how reading and writing go hand in hand and discusses the physical and mental environments best for both. Idea-getting, special-effects motivation, and techniques for writing strong, well-plotted stories told with vivid, picture-making words are presented by actual teacher-student talk sessions. Other topics include research and creative report writing, poetry, journal keeping, and letter writing. Appendix A describes various types of writing workshops and conferences for children and gives plans for presenting a Read a Book-Write a Book Conference.

Appendix B lists books that we have found helpful and inspiring and that we recommend to all who are interested in writing. We have learned much from books such as Mauree Applegate's *Freeing Children to Write*, Ronald L. Cramer's *Writing, Reading, and Language Growth*, and Dorothy Grant Hennings and Barbara M. Grant's *Content and Craft*, and we have found excellent motivating projects and activities in books like Murray Suid's *Building Strong Writing Skills, I Wonder Whatever Happened to Amelia Pickett* by Connie Markey, and *The Good Apple Creative Writing Book* by Gary Grimm and Don Mitchell. Our handbook, however, devotes fewer pages to philosophies and theories than the first group of books and more pages to actual techniques for teachers than the second group. We use talk sessions, a procedure found in none of the above books. We give plans and materials for presenting a children's writing conference, and we devote chapters to rarely covered subjects such as getting ideas, keeping journals, using special effects for motivation, and guiding children toward self-editing. We also include many quotations throughout the book, from the classics, from present-day teachers and authors, and from children's own writings. These quotations not only augment the ideas we are presenting, but also suggest selections to read aloud and to use for posters and illustrations. Quotations from the children's writings, especially, are intended to inspire other young writers.

Creative Writing is a work book—a *working* book. It brings a different dimension to creative writing with children because we, the authors, have been elementary school teachers and are professional, published writers of fiction and nonfiction, short stories and books. Combining the expertise, experience, and techniques of both teaching and writing, we bring a flexibility in finding ideas, a freedom in writing—a new approach—to creative writing handbooks. This book is for you, not only to follow the suggested techniques and talk sessions we present, but also to use as a springboard into your own ideas and inspirations. We want the material here to stimulate and encourage you to develop and create material of your own. We hope you will find new and exciting ways to use our suggestions. We are sure that the methods we have found successful in our teaching will be just as successful for you. With this book you will be able to help your students discover the pleasure and challenge of creating together with the satisfaction of accomplishment, and you will share with them the joy of writing.

Acknowledgments

Lloyd Alexander for material from "Wishful Thinking—or Hopeful Dreaming?" *The Horn Book Magazine*, August 1968, Vol. 44, No. 4. Copyright 1968 by Lloyd Alexander.

Coward-McCann, Inc. (a Division of Putnam Publishing Group). Quotation from *Linnets and Valerians*, text copyright © 1964 by Elizabeth Goudge, reprinted by permission of Coward-McCann, Inc.

Doubleday and Company, Inc. for material from *The Wolves of Willoughby Chase* by Joan Aiken, *The Girl's Journey* by Enid Bagnold, *Georgie* by Robert Bright, and *Hailstones and Halibut Bones* by Mary O'Neill.

Dover Publications, Inc., for material from *Creative Power* by Hughes Mearns, copyright 1958.

The Gunning-Mueller Clear Writing Institute for material from Robert Gunning, *The Technique of Clear Writing*, New York: McGraw-Hill Book Company, Inc. Copyright, 1952 by Robert Gunning.

Harcourt Brace Jovanovich, Inc., for material from *Language in Thought & Action*, Fourth Edition by S. I. Hayakawa, copyright 1978.

Hennings, Dorothy Grant for material from Hennings, Dorothy Grant, and Barbara Grant. *Content and Craft—Written Expression in the Elementary School*. Englewood Cliffs, N.J.: Prentice-Hall, Inc., 1973. Used with permission of Dorothy Grant Hennings. Hennings, Dorothy Grant, and Barbara Grant. *Written Expression in the Language Arts*, 2nd ed. New York: Teachers College Press, 1982. Used with permission of Dorothy Grant Hennings.

Horizon Press for material reprinted from *A Testament* by Frank Lloyd Wright, copyright 1957, by permission of the publisher, Horizon Press, New York.

The Horn Book, Inc., for material from Leonard Wibberley in *Horn Book Reflections*, Elinor Whitney Field (ed.). Copyright 1969, The Horn Book, Inc., Boston, Mass. Used by permission.

Alfred A. Knopf, Inc., for material from "Velvet Shoes," from *Collected Poems of Elinor Wylie*. Copyright 1932.

MD Publications, Inc. for material from "The Biology of Words" by Isaac Goldberg. *MD*, April 1968, Vol. 12, No. 4. Reprinted with permission from *MD* Magazine.

Charles E. Merrill Publishing Co. for material from *Children's Writing and Language Growth* by Ronald L. Cramer. Copyright © 1978.

W. W. Norton and Co., Inc., for material from Sarton, May. *Mrs. Stevens Hears the Mermaids Singing*. Copyright © 1965 by May Sarton. Sarton, May. *The House by the Sea*. Copyright © 1977 by May Sarton.

Pantheon Books, a Division of Random House, Inc., for material from *A Gift from the Sea* by Anne Morrow Lindbergh. Copyright © 1955. And from "Alms" from *The Unicorn and Other Poems*, Anne Morrow Lindbergh. Copyright © 1956.

Random House, Inc., for material from *Future Shock* by Alvin Toffler. Copyright © 1970.

Fleming H. Revell Company for material from *A Touch of Wonder* by Arthur Gordon. Copyright © 1974 by Fleming H. Revell Company.

Yale University Press for material from "Alone" and "The Drum," from *Songs for Parents* by John Farrar. Copyright 1921. Reprinted by permission from John Farrar, *Songs for Parents*, Yale University Press.

Viking Penguin Inc. for material from *Journey Outside* by Mary Q. Steele. Copyright © 1969 by Mary Q. Steele. Reprinted by permission of Viking Penguin Inc.

one

Why Write?

... My friend, the pencil.

I think children should write because it is the one activity which gives thought a concrete form which can be examined and improved upon.

A second reason is that good writing requires a heightened examination of one's experience of life, searching memories and recalling sensory images and details, as well as emotions. This process can lead children to a more complete awareness and sensitivity to the things they experience.

A final reason that I think children should write is simply that writing is a pleasurable and fulfilling activity. I am constantly amazed at how proud children are of their writing and at how much they want to share with others what it is they've written. Writing seems somehow to be a natural human activity which allows us to express ourselves and to share that with other human beings.

Noel Pazour
Former Content Area Resource
 Teacher
Elementary Language Arts
Boulder Valley Schools,
Colorado

WHAT IS CREATIVE WRITING?

What is creative writing, and why should we teach it? There is some argument that "creative writing" is a misnomer because all writing is creative; that it may be good writing or bad, but it is still creative writing. Perhaps what is really confusing is the way we use the term *English* in today's curriculum. Someone has suggested that English is a made-up word meaning *writing what the teacher wants to read*. Do students feel that they must write only to please others, that they have to write things that will draw praises from adults? If so, then here is where we'll find our definition for creative writing: It is the writing we *want* to do rather than the writing we *have* to do.

FIVE DISCOVERIES

The Opportunity for Expression

> So much of a child's schooling is *being told*. Writing, and creative writing in particular, gives children an opportunity to grow, to unfold, to express their thoughts and feelings. Writing gives children a means of communicating with the world—a dialogue between each child and eternity.
>
> > Judith Girard
> > Reading Specialist
> > Jefferson County Public Schools,
> > Colorado

One of the first reasons for encouraging children to write is to give them the opportunity to express and communicate their thoughts and ideas. When children discover they can write freely and independently about things they think and feel, they will have taken a giant step, not only into the world of writing but into the world of themselves. Writing is rather like talking to oneself. It allows one to relive and rethink experiences and helps to give shape and perspective to original ideas. It helps children to become acquainted with the person who lives inside them. Heather, in fifth grade, said, "I feel when I'm writing I'm experiencing myself."

The Importance of Being Able to Communicate

A second discovery we want children to make through their writing is the need to communicate clearly. Teaching creative writing is not just giving them the chance to put down thoughts, it is also teaching children to say what they want to say in a way that others will be able to understand. This includes their learning about grammar and punctuation and the structure of sentences and paragraphs. It also includes learning about the power—and pleasure—of words. It means making children aware of what good writing is by sharing the material of published writers as well as that of their peers.

Dr. Norma J. Livo, Professor of Education at the University of Colorado, Denver, tells us,

> The sight of the faculty mailboxes filled with notes, memos, and other bits of communication, triggered the thought. There they were—full and messy—sort of like our thoughts and minds.
>
> I see writing as a method of organizing our ideas and observations. If we write our ideas and read what we have floating around in the mailboxes of our minds we can study our own thinking with more clarity.

Children need to see writing as a challenge that is full of surprises. We must encourage children constantly in writing so that they will have air mail stamps on their ideas instead of having them bound for the dead letter office.

The Therapy of Writing Down One's Thoughts and Feelings

Children can also discover the therapy or catharsis of writing in order to relieve emotions and feelings, even ones they fear are not proper or acceptable. Trust has to be established between child and teacher, however, before the child is likely to have the courage to expose or share thoughts. And adults can gain understanding and insight to children's needs through what those children put down on paper. Donovan, in sixth grade, wrote,

> *Pencil racing along my page*
> *Spilling out my sudden rage....*
> *Swirling with happiness...*
> *My friend—the pencil.*

The Awareness of One's Own Creative Ability

A fourth reason for teaching writing skills is to help children discover their own creative abilities. Our children are being bombarded with other people's ideas and thoughts and creations. Statistics tell us that children have already watched from five thousand to eight thousand hours of television before they ever start kindergarten,[1] and by the time they finish high school they have put in eighteen thousand hours or more with television as compared with twelve thousand hours at school.[2] Statistics also show that 98 percent of all American homes have television, that their owners spend as much as twenty-three hundred hours in front of their sets each year,[3] and that many of them spend more time at their sets than they do at any other activity except earning a living and sleeping.[4]

In fact, whatever way people choose to spend their leisure time, it is most likely to be a consumer activity: if not looking at television, then watching sports events or movies, listening to music, reading. And, of course, there is nothing wrong with these pastimes—except that the consumers, children or adults, may never become aware that they can be producers, creators, as well.

As children write they will learn to recognize ideas all about them that can be turned into stories or plays, poems or journal thoughts. They will find that they can say something in a way no one else does because each of them sees in a way no one else does. They will discover that they can create, out of their own ideas, something of worth to share with others.

The Fifth Discovery

I think children should write because it provides an opportunity for each student to gain increased awareness of the beauty, "magic," and power of language. Through creative writing, students engage in divergent thinking; personal ways of looking at the world are legitimately expressed and, at times, communicated to others. And, of course, the feeling of personal worth which is fostered makes creative writing a must in every classroom.

Phylliss J. Adams
Professor of Education
University of Denver

When children have learned that they are able to present their ideas to others in a competent manner; that they can express their personal feelings to help others or themselves; that they, being unique, have a way of seeing and a way of saying things that belongs to no one else; then we hope the fifth reason for writing will be evident. It is simply that children may find pleasure in the challenge of creating and in the satisfaction of accomplishment—that they may discover for themselves the joy of writing.

NOTES

1.   Joan Anderson Wilkins, *Breaking the TV Habit* (New York: Charles Scribner's Sons, 1982), 12.

2.   Kate Moody, *Growing Up on Television* (New York: Times Books, A Division of Quadrangle/The New York Times Book Co., Inc., 1980), 5.

3.   Wilkins, *Breaking the TV Habit*, 12.

4.   Gregg A. Lewis, *Telegarbage* (Nashville: Thomas Nelson, Inc., Publishers, 1977), 19.

two

Writing and Reading

And play at books that I have read ...

There, in the night, where none can spy,
All in my hunter's camp I lie,
And play at books that I have read
Till it is time to go to bed.

These are the hills, these are the woods,
These are my starry solitudes;
And there the river by whose brink
The roaring lions come to drink.

Robert Louis Stevenson,
The Land of Storybooks

Our ideas are based on our experiences, outward, inner, or vicarious. As preparation for writing we must help children to recognize, interpret, and use their own day-by-day activities, their wondering and daydreaming, and the shared happenings of others, whether witnessed firsthand or found in books. Some experiences can best be understood when discovered first in reading: *Empathy, self-understanding, values, and wonder* are four, and they lead the way to a fifth — *expression.*

The experience lies within the child but usually it takes an outside spark to help the child express it. Thomas Carlyle believed that the best effect of any book was its ability to excite the reader to self-activity. Sharing vicarious experiences, real or created, can be the spark that inspires expression. Reading leads to writing.

EXPERIENCE WITH A CAPITAL E

Ideas for creative writing come from Experience: Experience spelled with a capital E. That is what books, articles, and speakers on the subject of creative writing have told us, over and over. But how many children, how many of us adults, recognize Experience in our own day-to-day lives? Aren't we inclined to believe that adventures happen to heroes and heroines — at least to other people — never to us? And don't we usually feel that the happenings in our ordinary lives are too uninteresting to share?

But in defining the word *experience* the dictionary uses terms such as *encounters, tests and trials, participation, understanding.* What better way can we find to recognize, to consider, and to evaluate our encounters and to reach an understanding of them than by sharing?

Of course, the larger and better cultivated the field of experience, the greater the harvest will be. So it is up to us to encourage our children to stretch the boundaries of their fields and to know and appreciate what is growing there. First, we must help them recognize the experiences of their everyday lives — with the people they meet, around their neighborhoods, during their work and play. We should also teach them to appreciate the world of their wondering and dreaming, because imagination is experience, too. Then we must provide them with vicarious experiences through hearing about the lives, adventures, feelings, and thoughts of others.

Listening to Lucy's story about her dog, Foxy, can help another child to realize that his cat or gerbil or guppy is material for a story. Steve's description of his first train ride might inspire others to tell of plane rides, raft trips, or even roller coaster adventures. And there are many more, many deeper experiences than these to be shared, with no better way to find them than by reading.

Empathy

The first of these experiences is learning about the feelings of others; being glad or unhappy or concerned by what happens to someone else. Mary, age eight, spent all of a hot July afternoon in her room reading. When called for supper she came down the stairs reluctantly, her eyes red. Her mother asked, "Mary, have you been reading too long?" "No —" There was a pause. "Charlotte just died."

Self-understanding

The second experience follows naturally after this. Readers recognize and identify their own feelings in the emotions of those they read about. They learn to relate the expression of other people's feelings to their own.

Henry Wadsworth Longfellow wrote in "The Children's Crusade,"

> *Other feet than yours have bled*
> *Other tears than yours been shed,*
> *Courage! Lose not heart or hope.*

Values

> Men must have at least three dimensions to have a full life
> and those dimensions are Past, Present, and Future.
>
> Leonard Wibberley[1]

The third experience in the encounter with books is the learning about our heritage of values. Children need to know what has happened before they were here and to speculate about what will happen in the future. They need heroes. They need to see both faults and virtues acted out simply. Experience too strong, too emotional, to be told in realistic stories can be presented in fantasy, allowing — encouraging — children to relate with heroes and forces of goodness and justice. "Young children yearn for values; the younger they are, the clearer they want those values to be," Lloyd Alexander says. He continues,

> They crave true heroes, not antiheroes (they can find out about them later); they have a taste for justice, mercy, and courage, which may be naive and unrealistic to adults. But they will have time to puzzle over the complexities and ambiguities of these virtues in the real world. Indeed, without the simplicities first, they may be ill-prepared to deal with the complexities.[2]

Wonder

The fourth experience through reading is the development and cultivation of imagination and curiosity. Call it wonder or awe or amazement, it is an ability children have but that is all too often lost as people grow older. Wonder is the gift of recognizing the extraordinary in the seemingly ordinary, of seeing the world through a prism. It is also that reaching out toward the world of fantasy and faery; a wishfulness and dreaming strong in childhood, with haunting wisps and nostalgic glimpses carrying over into adulthood, a longing for the golden days ... that never were. Kenneth Grahame, through his character Mole, captures this spirit of wonder in the opening lines of *The Wind in the Willows*:

> Spring was moving in the air above and in the earth below
> and around him, penetrating even his dark and lowly little
> house with its spirit of divine discontent and longing.

These four experiences, *empathy, self-understanding, values*, and *wonder*, in whatever form they come, with whatever emotions they come, lead the way to the fifth experience, *expression*. Here children can express their own feelings of sorrow, delight, terror, victory, anguish, compassion, wonder, or longing by methods of their own creation.

THE TINDER BOX

The experience, limited or wide, lies within the child. But children will probably need something from outside themselves to help them use and express experiences. A spark of inspiration? Let's consider that spark for a moment.

In old days people carried tinder boxes which they used to start their fires. The dictionary tells us, tinder box: a metal box in which tinder is kept, usually furnished with a flint and steel for producing a spark

and

tinder: something very inflammable, esp., such a material used for kindling fire from a spark

and

spark: an ignited or fiery particle such as is thrown off by burning wood, or produced by one hard body striking against another; that which, like a spark, may be kindled into a flame or action

The spark does not happen spontaneously or by wishing, but comes from an already burning fire or by flint and steel striking together. Occasionally, one's own rousing adventure or emotional encounter may be great enough to throw out the spark necessary to light the tinder that is our imagination and our longing to create. But more often it takes flint and steel; someone else's idea, anecdote, description, use of a word, to strike against or make contact with a personal experience of our own. The spark is then created, the tinder is lighted, and our experience is "kindled into a flame or action."

LET'S READ

In a very real sense, people who have read good literature have lived more than people who cannot or will not read.... It is not true that we have only one life to live; if we can read, we can live as many more lives and as many kinds of lives as we wish.

S. I. Hayakawa[3]

Reading for Profit and Pleasure

Every day should have some reading for pleasure; at home and at school, reading to one's self and being read to. These reading periods are for enjoyment, not for structured lessons, and they should never, *ever*, be withheld as discipline or punishment.

For readers and listeners alike the reading-aloud period can also provide many benefits besides pleasure and relaxation.

Technically, hearing good writing read aloud will

increase and enrich vocabulary
demonstrate specific uses of words
illustrate development of ideas

Inspirationally, it will

> develop recognition of experience
> spark imagination
> give courage to experiment in writing

In considering purpose as well as pleasure for the reading-aloud period keep in mind the variety of materials to choose from:

> fiction or nonfiction
> realism or fantasy
> here-and-now or historical subjects
> poetry or prose
> whole books or excerpts

In addition to ideas and concepts, reading aloud can demonstrate the use of

> language patterns and imagery
> rhythm and rhyme
> alliteration and repetition
> onomatopoeia
> mood-creating words

More on words and word use is found in chapter 7.

Imitation

To worry that by providing children with models of good writing we'll encourage imitation and so discourage originality is to forget that imitation is basic in learning. We learn to speak by copying speech, to form letters by copying letters.

Children absorb what they hear and see and read, but unless we specifically say, "DO AS I DO" they are usually unaware of imitating. If you read *Chicken Soup with Rice* to your class and then ask them to write poems, yes, you'll get a lot of poetry flavored with chicken soup and rice. But with encouragement they'll move beyond their close imitating, and as they gain confidence and experience they will develop their own forms of originality—their own style. And keep in mind that many professional writers admit to "being influenced" by some other writer along the way.

Notebooks

> "The horror of that moment," the King went on,
> "I shall never, *never* forget!"
> You will, though," the Queen said, "if you don't
> make a memorandum of it."

Lewis Carroll's White Queen was quite right. Things not written down are all too often things lost.

Older children should be encouraged to keep notebooks of words, phrases, sentences, ideas that they come across and like, both their own and those of other writers. They should learn at the very beginning to note the sources of the entries they make—author, title, page number at the very least. And it is never too soon to explain to young writers the difference between being inspired by someone else's ideas and copying those ideas and calling them one's own. Better that they learn early rather than late the meaning of the word *plagiarism*.

FROM READING TO WRITING AND BACK AGAIN

Reading as inspiration for writing can come full circle to writing as inspiration for reading. When you've studied music or dancing or acting you have more appreciation of the achievements of the professional musician or dancer or actor. You know how hard that person has worked to make it all seem effortless. And so with writing. When people begin to write they become more aware of what they read. That doesn't mean that a fifth grader is going to delight in analyzing Lloyd Alexander's paragraph structure or look for symbolism in *The Hardy Boys*. But having once tried to *tell* a story, that fifth-grader may well go beyond just the enjoyment of reading to the appreciation of a good story and to the curiosity about how the author has accomplished it. The more one writes, the more discerning one's reading becomes.

NOTES

1. Leonard Wibberley, quoted in Elinor Whitney Field, ed., *Horn Book Reflections* (Boston: The Horn Book, Inc., 1969), 353.

2. Lloyd Alexander, "Wishful Thinking—or Hopeful Dreaming?" *The Horn Book Magazine*, Vol. XLIV, No. 4 (August 1968), 389.

3. S. I. Hayakawa, quoted in Laurence J. Peter, *Peter's Quotations* (New York: The Viking Press, 1983), 7.

three

Creating a Good Environment for Working

Even when I'm not working I'm working.

"A Blank Page"

A blank page,
Staring up at me
laughing because I cannot think.
A blank page—
My pencil will not write,
stalling and breaking its neck.
A blank page....

Madeleine Cohen
Sixth Grade

"Childhood is the period of maximum creativity," Ashley Montagu tells us. "Play, imagination, make-believe, daydreaming, reverie, and fantasy ... are precursors of creativity in ... later life."[1]

But another observer warns, "Tests have shown that at the age of five, ninety percent of us measure high creativity. By the age of seven, the figure has dropped to ten percent and in adulthood to two percent."[2]

According to these gloomy figures it is obvious that our creativity isn't going to go very far or last very long unaided. Creativity, in order to grow and develop, needs the inspiration and exhilaration of many experiences. It also needs a nurturing environment that will encourage wondering, imagining, and experimenting. This environment is both physical and mental—the physical including time and place (or space); the mental, motivation and trust.

CULTIVATING CREATIVITY

Time and Place

It isn't easy to put one's thoughts and imaginings into words. It is even harder to put those words onto paper, especially when thoughts come faster than hand can write them down and when words are hard to spell. Writers need privacy, quiet, and time and space to think. How can this happen in a busy, crowded classroom?

First, by *making* quiet times. The teacher can create an atmosphere, a mood of thoughtfulness by reading aloud, encouraging a reflective sharing of thoughts and feelings, and then allowing a period of time in which everyone—including teacher—thinks and writes. Peggy Brogan, in "The Case for Creativity," speaks of a rhythm of exploring and considering: "Reach out ... pause ... make contact ... pause ... create meaning...."[3]

There should also be room in which to write: out-of-the-way places, as well-defined as a Creativity Corner, or as improvised as behind a screen or under a table, where children can go to write, undisturbed and undistracted, when other activities are going on. Remember, a lot of a writer's writing is being done when he looks as if he is wasting time, staring into space, daydreaming. As Marc Chagall is purported to have said, "Even when I'm not working I'm working."[4] Before they put pencil to paper writers have to *think*. No one can hope to be very creative in just the last five minutes before the bell rings.

Motivation

A congenial atmosphere for writing also provides inspiration—not just ideas for writing, but the wanting to write. We frequently feel that our own lives are too ordinary to write about. Reading aloud to children can encourage them to share experiences. Hearing the imaginative language of others helps stimulate their own imaginations. It can give a listener the courage to experiment with words, to begin to think in similes and metaphors. After hearing Humbert Wolfe's comparison of the sitting squirrel to a small grey coffee pot, will squirrels ever seem quite the same to us again? Lara, in sixth grade, wrote, "He slept like an old rocking chair, creaking with every breath." Listening to the ideas of others also opens up new vistas in both the world of facts and the world of imagination. Whether children agree or disagree with what they hear, they will begin to look at their world from different angles.

> Originality does not consist in saying what no one has ever said before, but in saying exactly what you think yourself.
>
> James Stephens

Inspiration and motivation have to extend to the uninterested writer and the non-writer, also. This may mean sitting and talking with them, taking down what they have to say, then letting them see what their own words look like, typed or written out. With very young children, schoolmates from upper grades might act as scribes. Using a tape recorder could give older children the sense of freedom and accomplishment they need.

Trust

The fourth of these elements of a good writing environment is *trust*, and, we might add to that, *courage*.

Hughes Mearns, in his book *Creative Power*, wrote, "It is not enough to discern a native gift; it must be enticed out again and again. It needs exercise in an atmosphere of approval. Above all it must be protected against the annihilating effect of social condemnation."[5]

Encourage your writers to speak up, speak out. Express what is uniquely theirs to say. No one else can see it, feel it, say it, in exactly the same way. But, when we encourage them to write honestly and specifically, then we must protect them. Children's creative expressions are largely confessional. Whether their writing is personal or to be shared, their privacy and their confidence *must* be respected. Nor should children's ideas, ways of saying things, ways of seeing things, be made fun of, or even inadvertently discouraged or put down.

Children's perspectives are different from adults'. They should be encouraged to look at the world about them and then to share their impressions and feelings. Myra Cohn Livingston has written, "We, as adults and teachers, teach honesty in matters of morals and ethics to our young people, but we are often apt to quash the honesty when it comes to the expression of feelings."[6]

And, if they are to share their thoughts, children will have to develop a trust among themselves, understanding, appreciating, valuing, one another's ways of seeing and considering things.

Wouldn't it be wonderful if we all could learn to look at other people's ideas as discoveries to think about, instead of as ridiculous notions to laugh at? If children are to develop the courage and confidence to put their ideas down on paper, then adults must not disparage those ideas, classmates must not make fun of them, and—too often overlooked—children must not be allowed to belittle themselves or their own thoughts.

THE EXTRA ELEMENT

If we are to keep their creativity alive and growing, we must see to it that our children have time and space, encouragement and confidence, to work at it. There is a fifth gift that adults can give to children, too. They can, that is, if they have cultivated the gift within themselves. It is the ability and opportunity to enjoy being alone. This is a blessing to anyone who has learned to develop it, a requisite for the creative person.

First, children must learn that being alone does not necessarily mean being lonely. Loneliness can be sad, but solitude can be a joy. May Sarton says, "Loneliness is the poverty of self; solitude is the richness of self."[7]

Today there aren't many window seats and apple trees, attics and vacant lots, where children can go to be alone. With after-school activities, music, dancing, karate lessons, TV programs, and paper routes, there aren't enough hours to go around. An over-programmed child doesn't have time to think. And children need time and place for solitude, for looking, listening, sitting, dreaming, for *thinking*. They need adults' encouragement and trust to know that it is all right to do these things.

Sylvia Link is the author of a poignant story about a boy who wanted the time "to see a tree grow." Arthur Gordon, in *A Touch of Wonder*, tells of a memorable hiking trip with his father.

> *We explored a cave, and at one point far underground snapped off our flashlights and sat there in darkness so profound that it was like being in the void before the beginning of time. After a while Father said, in a whisper, "Listen! You can hear the mountain breathing!" And ... I did seem to hear, in the ringing silence, a tremendous rhythm that haunts me to this day.*[8]

In her book, *Gift from the Sea*, Anne Morrow Lindbergh writes that we seem so frightened of being alone that we choke our space with continuous music, chatter, and companionship. "When the noise stops there is no inner music to take its place." She adds, "What a commentary on our civilization, when being alone is considered suspect; when one has to apologize for it, make excuses, hide the fact that one practices it — like a secret vice!"[9]

Developing an appreciation for what Wordsworth called the bliss of solitude, the chance to be alone with one's thoughts and dreams and fantasies, can prepare a child, can prepare us all, for handling the loneliness that is inevitable in every life. And, conversely, with the inner resources developed by solitude, we can cope, can provide for ourselves mental *lebensraum* when we find that the world is too much with us. What a blessing to give our children — the joy of Stevenson's starry solitudes, the ability to be one's own good company, to think, to dream, or even to watch a tree grow.

> *I want to explore all alone,*
> *With nobody spying around,*
> *All alone! All alone, all alone!*
> *It has such a wonderful sound.*
>
> John Farrar,
> *Alone*

NOTES

1. Ashley Montagu, *Growing Young* (New York: McGraw-Hill Book Company, 1981), 159, 163.

2. Ardis Whitman, "Children Need a Hiding Place," *Woman's Day* (April 1974), 152.

3. Peggy Brogan, "The Case for Creativity," *Creativity in Teaching*, editor Alice Miel (Belmont, Calif.: Wadsworth Publishing Company, Inc., 1961), 17.

4. Marc Chagall as quoted by Garson Kanin, *It Takes a Long Time to Become Young* (Garden City, N.J.: Doubleday and Company, Inc., 1978), 21.

5. Hughes Mearns, *Creative Power* (Mineola, N.Y.: Dover Publishing Company, 1958), 268.

6. Myra Cohn Livingston, *When You Are Alone/It Keeps You Capone* (New York: Atheneum Publishers, 1973), 66.

7. May Sarton, *Mrs. Stevens Hears the Mermaids Singing* (New York: W. W. Norton and Company, Inc., copyright 1965 by May Sarton), 183.

8. Arthur Gordon, *A Touch of Wonder* (Old Tappan, N.J.: Fleming H. Revell Company, 1974, Guideposts Associates, Inc., Edition), 197.

9. Anne Morrow Lindbergh, *Gift from the Sea* (New York: Pantheon Books, A Division of Random House, Inc., 1955), 42, 50.

four

Helping Children Get Ideas

*Everything has been thought of before,
but the problem is to think of it again.*

paper
white, clean
untouched, unused, waiting
lines, eraser, pencil, pen
scribbling, scratching, scheming
messy, inky
poem

Diane McConkey
Age thirteen

Ideas are all around us. Seneca says the best ideas are common property. But a writer knows how to recognize story potential. On hearing something, reading something, most people think, yes, that's interesting. A writer says, "Aha, that's a story."

Everything writers see, everything writers read, hear, taste, feel, is tucked away inside them. Sometime they will use it in a story. Writers take facts, mix them with feelings, and they have a story. It is these feelings that make a story unique.

As a teacher you can help children get ideas. One idea, talked over by thirty children, will result in thirty different creations, because each child is different, with different feelings, different experiences. The way a child will use his imagination to flesh out an idea, a story skeleton, will make it his story, the only one that child could write.

There is a theory that there are no new ideas. That everything has been thought before. Perhaps this is true. But I have not thought of it; *you* have not thought of it; to each student it is new. And filtering an old idea through each individual's personality is how new stories result.

Children love to write wild fantasy stories, the plot ideas vaguely resembling, or sometimes copying, today's TV programs and adventure movies. Point out copies, but let them write to get rid of the junk inside them. Encourage them to use their imaginations and praise strong fantasy stories. Then, as often as possible, ask for realistic fiction, stories that could happen to them. Introduce the different fiction genres—fantasy and science fiction, historical, western, romance, animal (true-to-nature as different from talking animals), and mainstream, which includes realistic and humorous fiction—and practice writing in each category to get children out of ruts.

Many children will not know how to develop an idea once they get one. An idea is like a seed. No writer gets a whole story at once. Writers get a seed which they plant in their minds. It takes time to grow. Maybe they will add water (techniques) and plant food (imagination). Then they get a better story. After the idea has grown, sometimes for a long time, the story comes to full bloom. This is the time to write it down.

There are idea helpers to aid in developing an idea. We call them Magic Words.

Magic Words

What if?
I wonder....
Why?
How?
Who else?
How did he feel?
And then what happened?

TALK SESSIONS

Throughout the book we use talk sessions to help children get ideas. We feel that no writing session should be started cold, giving an assignment with no warm-up period, no time given to "inspiring" the students. Teachers use this beginning time to talk students into having and developing ideas and into writing with enthusiasm.

Some children always have good ideas. It is during these talk sessions that these idea people can share, acting as models for children whose imaginations are not as well developed, or for those who have been discouraged and have let their senses get rusty. Perhaps we can even risk saying that in most classrooms, children learn more from each other than they do the teacher. Taken correctly, this statement relieves one person from the burden of being "know-all, see-all" to thirty students, and gives students more responsibility for their own learning.

In a talk session teachers start the conversation and keep it going, adding their own ideas, but for the most part, they use the idea helpers to pull conversations from the children. Some children will dominate the talk. You can try to pull in shyer students when you see they have something to contribute.

In the talk sessions illustrated in this book, children give ideal answers. At first your children's answers may not show much imagination and thought. Keep them talking until you get some original thinking. Praise the original idea, accepting the ideas that copy recently popular movies and TV shows, but staying with the session until you get better responses.

Children should always feel free to choose the form of their writings unless you are concentrating on one way of expression, but if a child always writes poetry, encourage him to write some prose and vice versa. Some young children's stories may even be arranged in poetry form, since a young child is very free with imagery, metaphor, and simile.

After a talk session we encourage the teacher to write when the children start to write, acting as a model. Then the teacher might wander over the room to help children who are stuck. Some teachers stand at the board and spell words for young children so flow isn't interrupted. Older students can guess at spelling and look words up later. It may help to provide a first sentence for some children. Students whose writing skills are not highly developed or those who have difficulty with written language may need to dictate stories part of the time. Occasionally, older students might be invited to act as secretaries for the younger ones. Both the older and the younger child will benefit here, since the older child can experience the freedom of the younger's language. Using a tape recorder freely during writing sessions can also be helpful — to record initial rendering or to allow children to hear their own work, especially their poetry.

Talk sessions make writing easy, fun, and make children enthusiastic. No child says, "I can't think of anything to write about." Most children can hardly wait to get started.

IDEA SOURCES

Following are many different sources for a teacher and class to find stimulus for writing. These are not meant to be all the subjects about which you can write. We cannot say too often throughout this book, that we hope teachers will add to our material, use their own imaginations freely, find creative sources to get children excited about writing as fun and as an integral part of any school curriculum.

Ideas from the Weather

Many creative stories and poems have come from feelings about the weather. We all have these feelings. How do we express them? This talk session illustrates how a creative teacher can give a class something about which to write.

Talk Session

Teacher:	What's happening outside, class?
Children:	It's snowing!
Teacher:	Where does the snow come from?
Children:	The sky. Heaven. Frozen water. A big bird shaking its feathers.
Teacher:	Sharon suggests that snow looks like feathers. What else does it look like?
Children:	Cotton. White leaves. Frozen stars. Torn paper. Potato flakes. Lace.
Teacher:	How does a snowflake feel?
Children:	Light. Airy. Lonely. Cold.
Teacher:	What would a snowflake factory look like?
Children:	Elves cutting out designs. Mrs. Winter shaking pillows. A giant salt shaker shaking out snow. A machine that turns out patterns.

Teacher:	How would the machine sound?
Children:	Clank. Puff-puff. Shhh. Swish.
Teacher:	How does the snow sound when it falls?
Children:	There's no sound. Shhh. Fffft. Spttt.
Teacher:	How does the schoolyard feel to have snow falling on it?
Children:	Angry. Cooled. Cold. A new dress. A white fur coat. A white brrr coat.
Teacher:	How do animals feel when it snows? (Name specific animals.) Cities? Children? Mothers?
Children:	(Would respond to each question.)
Teacher:	What if it snowed all day? A week? Snowed and never stopped? Who could get it stopped? How?
Children:	
Teacher:	Would you like to be a snowflake? How would it feel?
Children:	
Teacher:	Let's write words on paper about snowflakes. You may write a story or a poem, whichever you like.

"Mrs. Snow"

Old Mrs. Snow is a widow, you see,
Who lives up on the clouds.
She has a bucket of lovely white flakes,
That sits in her fluffy white house.
And if a child says, "Please, Mrs. Snow,
*   I'd like some flakes."*
She takes her bucket and dumps them out,
And covers the world with snow!

Lisa
Age ten

Ideas from Your Backyard

Lots of children can write about very dramatic situations like avalanches, hurricanes, disasters, or exploring space, but there are also ideas in their own backyards. They do not have to travel thousands of miles away to get a story. Encourage them to look around their classrooms, their streets. Then use the Magic Words.

Talk Session

Teacher:	Who lives in your backyard?
Children:	Grass. Crickets. Spiders. Birds. Worms.
Teacher:	Do they know each other and work together? Do they get along?
Children:	Birds eat worms. Spiders catch crickets. They hide in the grass.
Teacher:	Can you think of a time when they might need to work together?
Children:	A flood? A party? Someone would make them all move?

Teacher:	What kind of a party would the residents of your backyard have?
Children:	A cricket could play the fiddle. A square dance. A spider could spin decorations. A mouse might bring refreshments. Cheese doodles. A bird could sing. They could have a talent show.
Teacher:	What could a worm do? How would he feel if he couldn't think of anything?
Children:	Sad. Awful. Left out. Maybe he could squirm. A worm squirm. That's funny.
Teacher:	What could a worm squirm be?
Children:	A game? A new dance? He could teach everyone a new dance.
Teacher:	Can you write a story or a poem about the party? Or the flood? Or something else that got them together?

Ideas from Material Teacher Reads Aloud

Choose passages from books to read that stimulate imagination. Nonfiction (adult or children's books) is often best for this type of exercise. For example, read this passage from *Future Shock*.

> Given our new, fast-accumulating knowledge of genetics, we shall be able to breed whole new races of blue people—or for that matter, green, purple, or orange.[1]

Now do a talk session. Ask these questions or others. What colors would people be? What problems would this cause? Would it be better if everyone in the world was one color? Or if everyone was a different color? I wonder how it would feel to be a purple person? How would we treat each other? Would some colors be more desirable than others? What if green people didn't like blue people? What if people were colored according to their personalities? What color would you be? What color would a happy person be? A coward? A bully? What if people changed colors like chameleons? What if the way you felt made you change color? What if a baby was born that was half one color and half another? If a yellow person and a blue person married, would they have a green baby? What colors would animals be? Write a story or poem about people colors.

"Yell-Io and Blue-Iet"

"Zabrina, I just won't let you see that boy. Don't say it, because we won't argue with you. He's a perfectly nice boy. It's just that we can't have you seen with a yellow person. Our friends will be embarrassed to be seen with us and there will be embarrassment all around."

"So," I yelled. "Friends and personal embarrassment are more important than your own daughter's feelings?"

They were being terrible and unfair. I hated them. All of this over a color. It was just silly!

When I grow up I'm going to let my kids see whoever they want, no matter what color that person is! I thought.

Then the full meaning of my father's words hit me. I would never be able to see or talk to Zorgany again! The tears began to flow, I couldn't help it. I felt a sob rising from my chest, and I tried to stop it, but it fought its way out. Then I was crying full blast. I couldn't stop. I felt a tear falling off my face and caught it with my hand. I wiped my eyes and they stayed clear just long enough for me to see the tear, crystal clear with no particular color.

Suddenly, I wished I was a teardrop. They were all the same color; no color, and never had time to love or hate. I flung it off my hand, mad at it for having the life I wanted.

Heather Aker
Age twelve

Read this passage from *Future Shock.*

The opening of the sea may also bring with it a new frontier spirit — a way of life that offers adventure, danger, quick riches or fame to the initial explorers. Later, as man begins to colonize the continental shelves, and perhaps even the deeper reaches, the pioneers may well be followed by settlers who build artificial cities beneath the waves — work cities, science cities, medical cities, and play cities, complete with hospitals, hotels, and homes.[2]

Toffler goes on to tell about Dr. Walter L. Robb, a scientist at General Electric, who has created an artificial gill, a synthetic membrane that extracts air from the surrounding water.

Indeed, the old science fiction speculations about men with surgically implanted gills no longer seem quite so impossibly far-fetched as they once did. We may create (perhaps even breed) specialists for ocean work.[3]

Talk Session

Do you think many people would want gills? Will some people live under the ocean some day? What problems would this cause? What fun could they have? What would life be like? What adventures would they have? What would they need to learn? What would going to school be like? What jobs would people have? What kind of trouble could a boy or girl get into? What pets would they have? Would you want to live under the ocean? Could you ever come back to earth? What things would you miss? What kind of home would you have? What would you eat? Wear? Write a story about someone living under the sea and his adventures. You may want to do some research to write your stories. If so, read all you can find about living under the ocean, then use your imagination to put yourself into the future and under the seas.

Other Suggested Readings

Dixon, Dougal. *After Man, A Zoology of the Future.* New York: St. Martin's Press, 1981.

Droscher, Vitus B. *The Friendly Beast.* New York: E. P. Dutton, 1971. (Discoveries in Animal Behavior.)

——————. *They Love and Kill.* New York: E. P. Dutton, 1976. (Courtship and Mating in Animals.)

Folsom, Franklin. *Exploring American Caves.* New York: Collier Books, 1970.

Idyll, C. P., ed. *Exploring the Ocean World.* New York: Thomas Y. Crowell Company, 1972.

Reader's Digest. *Marvels and Mysteries of Our Animal World.* New York: The Reader's Digest Association, 1964.

——————. *Our Amazing World of Nature.* New York: The Reader's Digest Association, 1969.

——————. *Story of the Great American West.* Pleasantville, New York: The Reader's Digest Association, 1977.

Rosen, Stephen. *Future Facts.* New York: Simon & Schuster, 1976.

Sagan, Carl. *Murmurs of Earth: The Voyager Interstellar Record.* New York: Random House, 1978.

Stern, Philip Van Doren. *Secret Missions of the Civil War.* New York: Bonanza Books, 1959.

Toffler, Alvin. *The Third Wave.* New York: William Morrow and Company, 1980.

Select sections from one of the above books or others of your choosing and read aloud to your students. Look for passages that would stimulate the imagination and lead to discussion. Let the writing grow out of the discussion.

Creative Assignment

Write a letter to tell an alien child what you and your life are like on earth. Imagine what he would write back.

Creative Assignment

Select an animal from Dougal Dixon's idea of future animals. These are based on real possibilities. Have children invent their own future animals either from imagination or how they think animals will progress and mutate. Invent animals from other planets or galaxies.

"The Slimegator"

Long, thin and purple.
1000 sharp teeth and good for watch dogs.
Eats hot rubber with A-1 Sauce. Weighs 300 pounds
  and loves birthday parties.
When I feel him he feels like liquid, but your hand
  doesn't get wet.
Ears sharp as pins.
Wears hat because disabled without it. If you take
  the hat off he is as sweet as a kitten.

Johanna Tomlin
Age ten

Ideas from Books or Magazines That Children Read

Reading is one of our favorite ways to get new ideas. Share with your students ways to turn their reading to idea-getting by using the Magic Words. Here are some examples from a sample class's reading.

Bob is reading a copy of *Ranger Rick's Nature Magazine*. He finds an article about forest fires. Then he uses the idea helpers. How would an animal feel when he knew a fire was coming? What would he do? What if he got lost from his family? What experiences could he have? How would the fire feel to him? How would it sound? Bob can write this into a story.

The same article gives Sue another idea. She might say to herself, what if I was camping with my family and we saw/heard/smelled a forest fire coming? What would we do? How would I feel? How would we save ourselves?

Sam could get another story by saying, what if a friend and I were hiking and we saw a fire starting to spread from a campfire someone hadn't put out correctly? What if my friends wanted to try to put it out, and I knew the best thing to do was go for help?

Another article in the magazine tells how a mallard takes a bath. Rebecca wonders how other animals take baths. After more research she can write a creative science report. She could also write a story about a kangaroo rat who couldn't find any water in which to bathe so he bathed in sand, and that's why today all kangaroo rats bathe in sand. How about a kitten who didn't like to wash? What problems would she have? A chicken who bathes in dust and messes up someone else's appearance?

Mary reads the article about how a shearwater bird and a lizard share a burrow. She wonders what problems two animal roommates might have. How could they solve them? She learns more about animals who live together and asks, "Would you want to live with a porcupine? Who is a good animal roommate?"

James wonders what would happen if a hummingbird wasn't happy with his bill and wanted another. A fairy birdmother grants his wish to try other bills. James would have to read about other bird bills. While he is reading he comes across the southern folk tale about the rabbit who wanted red wings. He reads it to the class and challenges them to write about other animals who are unhappy with their body parts.

The Elephant Who Wanted a Bigger Tail
The Bat Who Wanted a Headlamp
The Penguin Who Wanted a Pouch
The Walrus Who Wanted a Fur Coat
The Giraffe Who Wanted to Climb Trees

> Remember: A WRITER IS A READER

Ideas from Newspaper Articles

The newspaper is full of odd, funny, or just interesting articles that would make good stories. Suggest to children that they can usually pass up the front page headlines. They need to search through the inside pages for the small articles tucked away in a corner. These are the human interest stories.

Give children a week to clip newspaper stories that might give someone ideas for her own story. Bring them to class and share, using the Magic Words (see page 26). At first share one article at a time. Each could start a writing session. Later pin good articles to the bulletin board and challenge students to use them for story starters.

George found this article about a giant spider.

Talk Session

What if a spider was loose in your town? How would you feel? How would people act? Would you help look for it? What might happen while you were searching? How would anyone catch it? Write this story from the spider's viewpoint. How would he feel? How did he get there? How could he get back home?

Giant Spider Eludes Britons

Agence France-Presse

LONDON — A giant spider whose bite could kill a child is terrorizing the town of Basildon, northeast of London.

The venomous insect arrived four days ago in a consignment of fruit and vegetables from South America and has so far evaded all efforts to trap it by truncheon-swinging police and courageous townspeople.

Police have issued a picture of the spider and warned that doors and windows should be kept shut until the menace is captured — dead or alive.

Mary brought an article about a professor who took his class on a field trip and they got trapped in a cave. Remind the class that the article is a story starter, not *the* story.

7 Explorers Rescued From Cave

LAFAYETTE, Ga. (AP) — A cave-wise professor and six students — trapped beneath a mountain for 29 hours by flash floods — kept warm with calisthenics, heated soup over a candle and traded jokes until rescue divers reached them.

The stranded party emerged bedraggled but chipper Sunday night after more than two days in a large underground cavern.

When the first diver finally pulled his way against the force of gushing water through a 2-foot high, 60-foot long tunnel to reach the stranded spelunkers at about 9 p.m. Sunday, the cavers were preparing to make their own way out.

"Two minutes later, we would have met them all down the cave," said Warren Moore, a 22-year-old student at Georgia Southwestern College.

The first to slog from the watery cave was Cheryl Gillis, 19, who collapsed into the arms of her mother, Canolia Gillis of Macon, one of several anxious parents who kept a fireside vigil at the cave mouth in remote northwest Georgia.

"Thank God she's safe," Mrs. Gillis sobbed.

"The first 200 feet was comparatively easy," said Larry Bean, the diver who first reached the party. Then came the 60-foot underwater struggle.

Once he found air on the far side, Bean shouted, "Is anybody home?"

"They started yelling, 'Hey, we're here! We're here!'" he said. He said the group was high and dry about 1,500 feet from the mouth of the cave. "They were standing together on a bank in a large-sized room," he said.

They told Bean that during the ordeal, "They huddled together in order to keep warm and they slept. The professor took good care of them."

Barry Beck, an assistant professor of geology at Georgia Southwestern College in Americus and an ardent cave explorer, led a group of 11 into the Pigeon Mountain cave at 11 a.m. Saturday.

Tony Able, 19, one of four cavers who escaped before rising waters fed by torrential rainstorms flooded the only way out, reported after his friends were rescued that they told him "it was exciting and they had a good time."

The rescued spelunkers were wrapped in blankets, given dry clothes and offered warm drinks to offset their lowered body temperatures. Within 15 minutes several were giggling and joking.

"Oh, peanut butter and jelly — thank you," Miss Gillis said when she was offered a sandwich.

The seven rescued cavers were whisked past reporters to Tri-County Hospital in Fort Oglethorpe, Ga., 33 miles to the northeast.

"We were kind of expecting exposure to take more of a toll than it did," Bean said.

Bean's successful effort was the third try to reached the trapped party. The others — late Saturday and at midday Sunday — were hurled back by the water's crush.

Beck said the party was "completely in control of the situation at all times." He added that none of the students doubted they would be able to escape the cave.

"The type of students who pick this kind of activity, they're self-reliant to begin with," he said. "Some of them jump out of airplanes just for kicks."

Beck said experience would give the students confidence from "just knowing you can handle something like this."

Rains let up at about 5 a.m. Sunday and the water began to subside, reducing the force of the water inside the tunnel.

When the party entered the subterranean world Saturday morning a light rain was falling and the water level in the cave only slightly higher than normal.

They explored for about six hours. Equipment problems forced two of the party to head back early — Beck's 13-yearold son, Eric, and 18-year-old Tony Johnson, son of acting Georgia Southwestern President Harold Johnson.

Talk Session

What if your class went on a field trip and got trapped somewhere? What were you looking for? Where did you go? Would weather play a part? Could there be a flood? A snow storm? A bus wreck? A tornado? How would each person in the story handle the emergency? Would some be scared, others helpful? Would everyone work together? Would anyone panic? Would some be natural leaders? Discuss how emergencies bring out the best and the worst in people. What if the leader got hurt? Lost? Trapped and couldn't be the leader? Who would take over? Would everyone follow a new leader? Remember not to have too many characters. How could you solve this problem? Maybe the whole class didn't go. Maybe one group got separated from the rest. Maybe it was your Scout troup or just a bunch of friends on an outing. Your family. Remember to say how the main character felt. Show how other characters felt. Try to put yourself in the role of the main character. What would you do?

Read about how other authors used this idea.

Corcoran, Barbara, and Bradford Angier. *A Star to the North*. New York: Thomas Nelson, 1970.

Donovan, John. *Wild in the World*. New York: Harper & Row, 1971.

Fry, Rosalie K. *Snowed Up*. New York: Farrar, Straus and Giroux, Inc., 1970.

George, Jean Craighead. *My Side of the Mountain*. New York: Scholastic, 1959.

Knudson, R. R. *You Are the Rain*. New York: Dell, 1978.

L'Amour, Louis. *Down the Long Hills*. New York: Bantam, 1968.

Mazer, Harry. *Snowbound*. New York: Dell, 1975.

Morley, Walt. *Canyon Winter*. New York: Dutton, 1972.

Roth, Arthur. *Two for Survival*. New York: Avon, 1976.

Southall, Ivan. *To the Wild Sky*. London: Angus and Robertson, 1967.

Southall, Ivan. *Hill's End*. New York: Archway, 1962.

White, Robb. *Deathwatch*. New York: Dell, 1972.

Creative Assignment

Each child clips an article. He puts it in his notebook and writes a list of questions that would help him or others to turn it into a story. He can then use it for a story himself or add it to a class notebook used by the whole class for story starters. (Try to have as many options in the Writing Corner as possible, all sorts of things students could daydream about when they have finished their regular work and want to do some extra writing.)

Ideas from Watching TV

It is possible to get ideas while watching television, but when both audio and visual images are supplied, one tends not to be as creative, not to need to think. A person's imagination is not stimulated. He becomes a TV lump. Good literature moves emotions while TV is more likely to manipulate emotions.

However, there are a few programs which are worth watching to get fiction or nonfiction ideas. Nature shows can supply enough information to incite a child to want to know more. We have gotten ideas from the news shows such as "PM Magazine" or any program that presents interesting people doing interesting things.

It would be worthwhile to have a class discussion about the pros and cons of getting story ideas by watching television. Perhaps those arguing "pro" could bring in examples of ideas they have gotten.

Brainstorming to Get an Idea

Everyone has experience or memories or expertise upon which to draw to get an idea. The technique of free association turns loose ideas. Practice doing this until the class understands the technique.

Talk Session

Teacher:	I will say one word. Say what comes to your mind immediately. Then say what comes to your mind when you hear what someone else says. Do not raise your hand, but speak out. It doesn't matter if what you say is silly. Sometimes good ideas bounce off silly ideas. Pretend we are bouncing a ball all around the room. But the ball is a word or several words. Bounce the ball quickly. Ready? Horse.
Children:	Riding. Horseback. Saddles. Cowboys. Branding irons. Brands. Where they came from. Does it hurt the cow? What if a cow doesn't have a brand? Cattle rustlers. Etc.

The class will usually move in one direction. This group could have easily come out with horse shows and competition, or flying horses, fantasy, and so on. If the ideas don't move quickly enough, suggest that the words are hot potatoes. Remind children not to stop to think, or stop to ask themselves, is this a good idea? In the above example the class stayed with one subject. Here is another example that shows moving through many subjects.

1. Stilts
2. Stilt birds
3. Stilt animals
4. Giraffes
5. A giraffe who had to make stilts to be like others
6. To be taller
7. Why would anyone want to be taller?
8. Circus performer
9. To paint a house

10. To reach something
11. Burglars on stilts
12. Why do we want to be like others?
13. Being popular
14. A girl or boy who would do anything to be popular
15. Stealing
16. Shoplifting
17. She had to shoplift to join a club
18. Getting caught
19. Fear
20. Overcoming fears

Point out to students that if they reach a dead end, they can bounce back up to spin off an earlier idea, such as number twelve bounced off number five. Many of the above ideas would make a good story. Explain that sometimes they will get only one idea. Other times they will have more than they need, but they can always save extra ideas in an idea notebook for future use. (Be sure children keep an idea notebook for capturing ideas before they get away. We think we'll always remember great ideas, but they vanish easily.)

Do several brainstorming sessions as a class to be sure children understand the idea. Point out how important it is to work quickly so the words come from way inside, from the right brain. Then have each child take a piece of paper and start with his own words or idea. Give the children one minute to see how many ideas or words they can come up with, or how many words in the list. Timing the exercise encourages quick thinking.

Read some of the lists aloud and see how a person's mind has moved about. Remember there is no wrong way to do this. An idea is not right or wrong. Good ideas come from silly ideas.

> *— the imagination is only free when fear of error is temporarily laid aside.*
>
> Alvin Toffler

Brainstorming with an Idea

This is somewhat like the talk sessions before a writing period except the class will work on one story together. This helps children learn how to turn an idea into a story for themselves. They learn to think about all aspects of a plot, or all the potential there is in the one subject they start with.

Talk Session

Teacher: Today we're going to write a story together. We need a seed — an idea. Let's think about hobbies. Can we get a story from thinking about someone's hobby?

Jane: I collect miniature cats.

Joe: I collect stamps.

Sally: I watch birds.

Gary: I play baseball.

Teacher:	Good ideas. We could do a story from any of them. But a story has only one idea. Let's try stamp collecting. Who knows more about stamp collecting?
Bob:	There are rare stamps.
Beverly:	Once a man was murdered because someone wanted a stamp he had.
Teacher:	Sounds as if we could have a mystery story.
Gary:	Yeah. A stamp could get lost.
Bob:	Or someone could steal it.
Teacher:	Who is our main character?
Sally:	A girl.
Bob:	A boy.
Joanie:	Maybe we could have twins.
Teacher:	Would a young person be likely to have a rare stamp?
Bob:	No. They cost a lot of money.
Rebecca:	You could find it in your grandmother's attic.
Mary:	You could have it and not know you had it.
Gary:	How could you not know it?
Teacher:	What if someone, the thief, hid it in your house?
Sally:	Or in your stuff. Maybe a backpack.
James:	I'd find it right away.
Sue:	He'd have to hide it better.
Teacher:	We need another piece of the idea.
Beverly:	A doll. He could hide it in a doll.
Bob:	Or some other toy.
David:	I have a good idea. In a bowling ball.
Gary:	How could you hide anything in a bowling ball? That's silly.
Teacher:	Remember, no idea is silly.
David:	My hobby is bowling. My dad gave me his old ball. A man plugged up the holes that fit my dad's hand and drilled new holes for my hand.
James:	He put the stamps in the old holes of the ball?
David:	Sure. Simple, but a really good hiding place.
Beverly:	The stamp would get squished and ruined.
David:	He'd have to wrap it round the plug carefully and put a plastic cover over it.
Joe:	So the glue wouldn't ruin it.
Teacher:	That's a good idea. Now we've used two hobbies. How could the story start?
Bob:	Someone is trying to steal David's bowling ball. An action beginning.
Rebecca:	And David wonders why. His ball is old and not worth much.
Sam:	The Mystery of the Old Bowling Ball.
Teacher:	Good. Good. We have our plot, our characters, and our beginning. Let's all write the story. Then we can share and take parts from each one to make a class story. We could even write it into a play and present it to Mrs. Brown's room.

Note: The class could continue to write the story or play together with one child as secretary, but this is very time-consuming. It also eliminates ideas from quiet children. Keep reminding the class that when brainstorming, no idea is too silly or dumb to toss out. Encourage them to let their minds wander freely. Many creative ideas were first thought to be silly. Many ideas and discoveries were accidents. A very important thing for children to learn is that it is all right for an idea not to work out. If we needed a guarantee that every idea we have will be wonderful, successful, and perfect, we'd never risk getting it. Starting over, erasing, scratching out, throwing out—all are integral parts of a writer's life. Unlike playing a tennis match or a football game, we can write a story and then rewrite, fix it, if it doesn't come out a winner the first time.

Creative Assignment

Challenge the children to brainstorm and get a plot from: unusual occupations, toys, how toys originated, unusual characters, games.

We highly recommend a book that uses a similar type of brainstorming and calls it *clustering*. It is a right brain method that taps the subconscious for ideas and words, feelings, similes, metaphors, anything you associate with the central word. When you have clustered around a subject, you have the ingredients of a poem or a short piece of prose. The book is Gabriele Lusser Rico's *Writing the Natural Way* (Los Angeles: J. P. Tarcher, Inc., 1983).

Another book that gives ideas for creative thinking and will give you exercises for helping children learn to problem solve and get ideas is Roger von Oech's *A Whack on the Side of the Head* (New York: Warner, 1983).

Ideas from Themes

Good stories have an underlying theme, a moral, although we don't care for that word. The story says something on a second level, the first level being the story itself. Many stories are written just to entertain, and this is certainly acceptable, especially for children writing. But we find that a realistic story, even when written by a young person, usually has a theme whether or not the author was conscious of its being there. In many the main character learns a lesson. Teach a child to hide this lesson in the work, just as an adult writer would do. No one really enjoys a finger-shaking story, one that is heavily moralistic.

Exploring a theme before you write a story can be done in either of two ways.

One. Start with a book or story already written. Example: *The Saggy Baggy Elephant*. (A Little Golden Book.) Read the story. Discuss how the elephant thought he looked different, and he didn't want to be that way. Talk about the steps he went through to find out that all elephants looked that way and that he was an elephant. There was a reason he looked that way. Now ask the children if they could write a story about another animal who looked different using the skeleton of the elephant story. How about a person?

You can get a new story by taking any story down to its skeleton and then fleshing it back out with a new main character in a new, but similar, situation. You can even write the story in the same step by step manner. This is called paralleling. It is legal and also often called creative plagiarism. While it is a useful exercise and may be very insightful to a child who has never been able to carry a story step by step from beginning to end, you will want to discourage a child's always plotting a story this way. Quite often a story started in this manner takes on a life of its own and takes off in a different direction.

Two. Start with the theme. Someone is unhappy with his looks and tries to do something about it. He discovers that this is just the look for him. How does he feel inside? Are people different on the outside? The inside? Can someone do something because of the way he looks that no one else could do? Will this make him feel better? Could the same be true of an animal?

Think of other themes around which to build a story. Use an Aesop's *Fables*, or a book of quotations for theme ideas. Here are a few to get a class started:

Honesty pays.

A person wishes to be like someone else only to find out that person is unhappy — isn't happy being himself — has the same problems.

Someone sets out to teach someone else a lesson and learns the same lesson himself.

Sacrifice for the sake of the team, family, class, friend.

To make friends you have to be one.

Ideas from *Story Starters*

Some children need a first sentence or paragraph supplied and then the story takes off for them. This would also work with titles, although the title for a story often doesn't appear until late in the writing or even after the story is finished. You can supply story starters, but also encourage the children to write first lines and drop them in a classroom box or grab bag. These starters should tease the imagination, be the kinds of openings that make readers have to keep reading. Many writers say that after a good beginning they keep writing to see what happens.

Suggestions for Story Starters

Rosalie dashed into the house. "Mother, Mother, guess what?" The house was quiet. Then Rosalie looked around. Her mouth flew open. All the furniture was gone. She ran to the kitchen. The table and chairs were gone. The cupboards were bare. She stopped at the door to her room. Slowly she pushed it open. Empty! No one was in the house. Everyone had moved away and left her behind.

Larry bounced into the house after school. He was starved! His mother was in the kitchen baking. "Hi, Mom," he said. "Can I have a cookie?"

"May I have a cookie," his mom corrected. Then she looked at him in a strange way. "I'm sorry," she said. "But I don't think I know you. Don't you have the wrong house?"

I woke up suddenly. What a dream! I rubbed my eyes. Then I heard the sound from my dream. *Errrk.* It was real. The window to my room was slowly rising.

Dan was late to school again. Quietly he opened the classroom door and scooted to his seat. It would be on the first row.

"Are you a new student?" The teacher's voice sounded funny. Kinda low and purry.

Dan looked up into huge black eyes. His teacher had blue eyes and brown hair. This teacher's hair was gray, and sticking out from the sides of her hair were soft, fuzzy ears.

The weekend started like many others. We go camping a lot. My job is to gather firewood, and I had started into the woods to find dead or broken-off tree limbs. I heard this peculiar noise. When I looked around....

"A party? Mary Gordon's giving a party? When is it?" I started to think of the new dress I'd bought on Saturday.

"Yes, didn't you get an invitation? She gave them out last Friday. Oh, you were absent weren't you?" Natalie tried to make me feel better.

That was it, of course. I wasn't here and she had my card in her desk.

Ideas from Suppressed Desires

One nice thing about being a writer is having adventures, vicarious experiences that you could never hope to have otherwise. Ask children to think of something they've always wished they could do. It doesn't matter if they could ever hope to do it; that's part of the fun. Maybe Mary has always wanted to be a mountain climber, and Bob has always wondered what it would be like to be a rock star. Rebecca dreams of being a model and Beverly a wildlife photographer. I write about mountain climbing and I'm afraid of heights, but I've read every book ever written on the subject. I have claustrophobia but have explored caves and been lost in one. You can live under the ocean and fly to the moon when you're the author. Shy children can be in charge and win over bullies; they can be elected to office and star in plays. Not much is impossible unless it doesn't fit the story, and children will find this exercise very satisfying. Here are some titles for starters:

The Day I Climbed Mount Everest
The Day I Rode an Elephant in India
David Dawson, Deep Sea Diver
I Live on the Moon
Sharon Bower Sets Swimming Record

Have the children write their stories pretending they are there. They may want to do some research so the stories will ring true. Ask them questions about the subjects they have chosen: What equipment will you need to climb a mountain? Dive in the ocean? How hard do you have to work? How do you feel? Are you afraid? Do you think you might not be able to do it? Do you get into any trouble? Write about your struggle. Who else is in the story? Does everyone in the story believe in you?

Ideas from Traveling

Most children go places on vacation or field trips. Look for ideas in a place. Have children volunteer places they've been and talk about them or brainstorm story ideas from a place. Encourage children to keep a journal when they are traveling. Ask them to write down what they see, hear, taste, smell. To write feelings about being there, images that come to mind, similes or metaphors they think of. They can also describe people they meet, and conversations they hear, and collect pictures, brochures, and maps for later use.

Here are some suggestions for talking about places students have visited:

To the Airport: What did you see, smell, hear? What if you got on the wrong plane? What if someone hijacked your plane? What if you landed in a strange place? What if you saw someone sneak on the plane? What if you heard a funny voice in your seatmate's carry-on bag? A funny noise?

Disneyland: What could happen on one of the rides? What if some of the Disney characters or strange people walking around were real? What if the roller coaster ran away? What if the boat in the pirate ride went in a tunnel and came out in a strange place? What if one of the wax figures in one of the exhibits was you?

Camping: What adventure could you have with an animal? What if you got lost? What if there was a natural disaster—earthquake, flood, storm? What if all the trees came alive? What if an eagle dropped you a message and before you could look at it a deer whispered for you not to read it?

Walk around the Block: Who could you see that didn't belong on your block? What if you saw a lion in Johnny's back yard? What if something strange landed on Mr. Smith's roof? What if two birds started talking to each other?

Death Valley: Tell the story of finding Death Valley as if you were on the trip. (You will have to do some research about the discovery.) What would it be like to run out of water on the desert? What if a baby burro followed you to your tent? What if you saw a strange light in the sky while you were trying to sleep? What if the temperature started to change?

The Big City Nearest You: What if you got to the city and it was deserted? You discovered someone your age living under a bridge or in a box in an alley? Your bus never came and you had only a bus token? It got dark in midday?

Ideas from Using Special Effects and Visuals

This topic is so varied and done in such detail that the entire next chapter has been devoted to it.

TEACHER IDEAS

We have found teachers to be among the most creative people we know. You will have many ideas for helping children find writing material. Don't be afraid to try them. Remember, it is all right for an idea not to work out. If you get equally poor work from most of the students, or most of them say, "I didn't like writing about this," then rethink your idea or throw it out in favor of a better one. The time will not have been wasted. We learn from every experience.

Brainstorm for writing ideas to use in the classroom. Trade ideas with other teachers in your building, in your district. A teacher should be a reader. You will get ideas from your own reading and experiences. How can you use these so that they have child appeal?

Remember: Ideas are all around you.
Enthusiasm makes an idea come alive.

NOTES

1. Alvin Toffler, *Future Shock* (New York: Random House, 1970), 179.

2. Toffler, *Future Shock*, 169-70.

3. Toffler, *Future Shock*, 170.

five

Using Special Effects as Motivation

Children: of all people ... the most imaginative.

> Children: Of all people ... the most imaginative.
> They abandon themselves without
> reserve to every illusion.
>
> Thomas B. Macaulay

Using special effects, records, pictures, drama, is not as much an artificial way to stimulate children to have something to write as some might think. Any exercise that gets creative juices flowing, motivates words on paper, refreshes memory, is valuable to the writer. In our own writing we use music to help us set a party scene, sound tapes to put us on the scene, slides to help us return to the setting of a story or book. We sometimes create moods by make-believe to help us write an emotional passage. Playing like you're with the main character helps you write realistically.

If a feeling of *being there* or immediacy is achieved by use of various techniques, the child will have an active experience. Then he will be unable to say "I have nothing to write" because he can set down what has just happened in his body and mind.

Following are techniques and activities that can be used at the beginning of a writing class. All of the exercises stimulate imagination or loosen memories. The writing flows up through those experiences a child has had and each piece becomes personal, unique. Each of us sees the world differently. When children discover their inner eyes and realize that their opinions have worth, they will not only delight in writing but grow in self-confidence and esteem. "*You* have something special to say" cannot be repeated too often to each student.

Many of the activities suggested here are multifaceted and can be broken down to cover several writing sessions. Often the best writing comes from a session with a narrow focus, but sometimes introducing and providing many choices will give children the freedom to overlay their own focus and interests. Teachers should try to be as creative and open in their presentation of the activities as time, interest, and age level allow.

SENSORY AWARENESS

One of the best ways for a writer to put the reader on the scene is to appeal to the senses. Suggest that students write down how things look, sound, feel, smell, and taste. Most writers tell how something looked, but the other senses are often forgotten. If I write that mother's kitchen smelled of yeast and spices, the reader is transported back to some kitchen of the past that smelled the same way and remembers these smells. The reader smells them again while reading of the imaginary kitchen, steps into the story, and experiences it. If I write of the patter of rain on a roof, you hear that sound from your memory and you are there.

Talk of words that paint sensory images. Encourage your writers to search for the best word for a sound, a word that feels like the object the character has touched. Sensory images and words go hand in hand.

Activities for Sound

Pencil and paper in hand, the class moves outside. Each child should sit alone and put on his *listening ears*.

Teacher: Write down each noise you hear. Don't just name the sound (a car is going by). How does the car sound? Does it rattle? Purr? Hum? If you hear a bird, does it chatter, peek, trill?

Allow time for children to shut out the big noises and start to hear the small ones. Stay outside and share what the students hear. Now is the time to talk about sound words, the scritch of gravel as someone walked on the sidewalk, the drone of a plane, the clink or chink of the ring on the flagpole, etc.

Continue the exercise as the group returns to the classroom.

Teacher: As you return, listen carefully to all the sounds you hear. Go to your seat and write them down. Discuss the noise of people walking. The swish of jeans, pad of tennis shoes, clop of clogs. Point out different sounds of feet on grass, walk, corridor, vinyl, etc. Relate these to a story.

Teacher: If you have a character walking, tell how he sounded. Don't say "Mary walked down the street." Say, "As Mary skipped down Main Street her clogs clip-clopped." Or use a simile. "Clip-clopped like a horse in the May Day parade."

Creative Assignment

Ask children to take their notebooks outside at night when they are home and list all the sounds they hear. Give them questions to answer: How are night sounds different from the ones heard by day? Does the night affect sounds? How? Again use sound words, "the soft hooo of an owl," "tap-tap-tapping of limbs on my window pane," "the chirp and chirrr of a cricket announcing bedtime."

Creative Assignment

Have children list their favorite sounds. Remind them to record not only the noise but also how it sounds: "the clink of ice in a soft drink," "the purr of a kitten." So many children say music. Ask them, What kind of music? How does it sound? As an assignment, have them write their favorite sounds into sentences they might find in a story so that a reader would hear those sounds.

scritch	crick	rap	fissle	crinkle
scratch	creak	tap	swish	crunch
scrunch	chirk	smack	whish	jangle
crunch	chirp	whack	zip	jingle
burr	chirrup	thwack	sniff	thud
chirr	rattle	whomp	snuffle	babble
buzz	clitter	whap	sputter	splat
clang	clatter	hiss	whoosh	splash
twang	clack	siss	wheeze	splosh
squeak	flutter	shush	squish	splatter
squawk	sputter	sizzle	crack	zing
screech	patter	fizz	crash	zap

Activities for Smell

Place small amounts of various pungent-smelling articles in small bags. Number the bags. Pass the bags around the class while each child writes how each smells. Use cinnamon, other spices, coffee, tea, turpentine, wintergreen, oils of various kinds (place liquid onto cotton balls), a new book, wood shavings, newsprint, plant leaves (crushed for maximum odor), fresh bread or yeast, orange peel, and so on. Have children write sentences about each smell and then use those sentences in stories to help their readers experience the odors they are writing about.

Creative Activity

Have children write a paragraph of description about a place telling only how it smells, putting the reader on the scene.

A barnyard
A cheese factory
A lumber mill
A furniture factory
A meadow in spring
A forest in fall
A wolf's den
A beach
A summer rain
A flower auction
A cave
An old house
A fruit cellar

pungent	acrid	stinky	fetid	fulsome
spicy	peppery	aromatic	noxious	yeasty
tangy	rank	perfume	malodorous	fusty
salty	gamy	sweet	rancid	frowzy
brine	brackish	savory	reeky	stuffy
piquant	smoky	musky	foul	moldy
sharp	stench	musty	vile	mildewed
reek	flowery	putrid	miasmal	

Activities for Touch

Use the same exercise as for smell but place swatches of cloth and pieces of things to touch in the bag. Use materials such as tree barks, sandpaper, sand, sawdust, potting soil, flour, velvet, corduroy, fur, smooth stone, volcanic rock, sponge, and so on. Each child will place a hand in the bag without looking, touch one or more objects, and then write some similes: rough as oak tree bark, ridged as corduroy.

Creative Activity

Two children work together. One is blindfolded, one is leader. Leader takes blindfolded person around having him touch various objects and describe or identify them. Do this both indoors and outside. Have children note how other senses take over after a time, and have them tell their partners what they hear or sense as well as what they touch. Be sure that partners trade places.

Creative Activity

Have children write a paragraph of description about a place telling only how it feels when they touch things. Their description should put the reader on the scene.

A weaving or cloth factory
A bed in a rich person's house (a poor person's)
An exotic animal contest
An old house
Rolling in a grassy field
Sleeping in a rocky campsite
A library
A greenhouse
A pirate's treasure trove
A queen's throne

flossy	gooey	pocked	tingle	throb
silky	plush	squishy	prickle	pound
fluffy	crumbly	squishy	sting	chafe
knobbed	chalky	stringy	tickle	twitch
scaly	mealy	bouncy	shiver	rankle

gritty	shaggy	rubbery	creep	numb
slimy	gossamer	wiry	itch	grate
sticky	nubby	brittle	smart	irritate
barbed	scratchy	crisp	ache	wince

Activities for Sight

Collect a box of familiar objects. Each child chooses one to describe fully as if he's never seen it before and then shares the written description with class while showing the object.

Teacher: Writers don't use a whole page of description for one thing. They put one line or a few into a story to call attention to an object. "Fluted seashells decorated the beach like ornaments." If they use several lines of description it is best to weave them into the action of the story. In your writing, try to make your descriptions fresh and unique. Make readers see something in a way they've never thought of or a description so apt that they say, "Yes, that's the way it looks."

Dilar expected something ugly and fierce the way he always imagined willimars to be. Now he drew in his breath. The great broad head with gleaming green eyes, the thick fur, cream and black and orange, the slow grace of its movements along the ledge where it walked—he could have watched forever. But the tiger, having glanced at the two men and the donkeys, with sudden lazy elegance flowed down to the ledge below and disappeared among some boulders.

Mary Q. Steele[1]

Collect a box of unfamiliar objects and let each child choose one to describe fully. By looking at the object he should decide what it might be used for. (Look in a tool box or find unfamiliar hobby equipment. Sometimes an antique tool is unfamiliar to a child.)

Have children describe an object (or an animal) as if they were aliens from another planet and had never before seen it. Remind them to use all five senses in describing it.

Something under the trees smelled wonderful; it made his mouth water though it was like nothing he had ever tasted. The smell seemed to come not from the greenery or from the bodies of the trees but from the small roundish pink and yellow objects which hung from them and sometimes fell softly to the ground.

Dilar picked one up and examined it. The skin seemed to his fingers to have tiny hairs all over it, but the object itself was soft and rather squashy. He squeezed gently and the skin split and juice spurted out over his hand. At first he was horrified, for he supposed this thing was living, but after a bit he concluded that since it had fallen from the branch it was probably dead.

Mary Q. Steele[2]

"Elephant As Seen by an Alien"

This big grey creature seems as if it has two mouths. One for long range and one for short. It has long white spears coming out of the short range mouth. This creature has four support beams that move. It also has a scrawny little tail and small wings on its head that have no apparent use. This creature is exceptionally large.

Rob Wehner
Age twelve

Remind the children to use good verbs for see and look:

watch	glimpse	gape	witness	observe
leer	gaze	goggle	spy	scout
glance	glare	ogle	note	reconnoiter
peek	glower	inspect	discern	scrutinize
peep	stare	view	peer	survey
gawk	squint	pore over		

EMOTIONAL AWARENESS

Various ways can be used to evoke a feeling or create a mood in the writer. Students then write about the mood. Just as sensory images put the reader into the story, emotions written into a story make the reader feel the story with the main character. Writers have to feel these emotions as they write. If I am writing a scene where my main character feels sad, I try to remember a time when I felt sad. I do the same with anger or surprise, fear or dread.

Here are some activities to make a child aware of emotion; to help her feel an emotion, observe what her body does when she feels this way. Again stress the difference between showing and telling. Tell children not just to say that someone feels sad, but to paint a picture of sadness using imagery and simile and metaphor, making the reader think, "My, she felt sad." Then the reader will remember sadness and feel this way with the main character.

Have the children look for passages in books that make them laugh or cry and study these pieces to see how the author evoked this emotion in the reader.

Use each emotion as a different activity because most children cannot experience many moods in one session. Leading them into one mood takes time and the rest of the class period should be used for writing.

Loneliness

You will try to create an atmosphere of loneliness in the room.

Talk Session

Teacher:	How many like to be alone sometimes? Do you have a place where you can be alone? In a tree? Under a bush? In the basement? Under your bed cover? A writer needs time to be alone. You get to know who you are.
Lucy:	We have five people in our family. There's no place to go.
Teacher:	Maybe you need to make a bargain with a neighbor who has no children. For sweeping the walks or raking the yard you can have a hiding place in her yard. If you are alone are you necessarily lonely?
Johnny:	No, loneliness is when you feel left out and you don't want to be.
Teacher:	Then you could feel lonely at a big party with lots of people there?
Rebecca:	Or in a classroom when you're the new kid.
Teacher:	What are some sounds that make you think of being lonely or alone?
Steve:	A train whistling in the distance.
Mary:	Rain falling softly on dry leaves.
Ben:	A foghorn on a misty beach.
Bob:	Wolves howling.
Gary:	Especially if you're camping and it's night.
Beverly:	Waves washing onto a shoreline or a beach.
Teacher:	What color is lonely?
Children:	Grey, lavender, pale blue, tan.
Teacher:	Let's compare being lonely with something else you see or hear. For instance I think loneliness is one shoe in the middle of the highway. Write down what you think loneliness is, like loneliness is a child who's lost a penny in a gum machine.

After writing and sharing the similes encourage children to write a poem or a prose piece about being lonely. Before the class writes poems or prose you may want to play music that sets a lonely mood. Use sound effect records with train sounds, wolves howling, crickets chirping, water sounds. Read poems about loneliness or being alone. Perhaps you will want to divide the activities and write several pieces or write poetry after one stimulus and prose after another.

When you hear the wind blow, you're lonely.
When you hear funeral bells you're lonely.
When you're all alone and sad, you're lonely.
When you see a dead tree, you're lonely.
And when the old man cries, you're lonely.

Robbie
Age thirteen

Why did the hour slow itself down?
Why did I imagine the clock saying good-bye?
Why did every car passing by sound like the
one to take me away?

Robbie
Age thirteen

I waited. No one would come, no one would call. They didn't care — I was only someone that they used to get help from on their homework. Why should they talk to me? They passed by, huddled in little happy groups, giggling over every word that was said. Stupid, I thought fiercely, they're just stupid. I don't want to be a part of them anyway.

I reached the school yard. They'll think you're new, I told myself. You've lived here all your life and you're still not a part of anything.

Diane McConkey
Age thirteen

"Loneliness"

Loneliness is an emotion you feel most in a crowd. Loneliness is seeing words on a page but not understanding what they mean. It is a grey, swirling feeling that spins inside time and inside your mind.

Emptiness is lonely, but perhaps it has other empty words and thoughts thrown in the atmosphere without the mouth that spoke them thinking. Loneliness was at the beginning of time and will remain longer than anyone will know or want to believe.

These thoughts I am thinking are lonely as are the words on this page. And loneliness is the cry of the Siamese, frightened at the thought of an empty house ... and never finding what he wants.

Laura
Age twelve

Alone Poems

Edna St. Vincent Millay. "This Door You Might Not Open"
Donald Justice. "Poem to Be Read at 3 a.m."
Frank O'Hara. "To the Harbormaster"
Boris Pasternak. "Parting"
James L. Weil. "A Coney Island Life"
Robert Wallace. "Moving"
James Tate. "Flight"
Lou Lipsitz. "Young Woman on Her Own"
(These poems may be found in *The Crystal Image: A Poetry Anthology.* New York: Dell Paperback, 1977.)

Robert Frost. "Desert Places"
Robert Frost. "Locked Out"
(Frost, Robert. *The Poetry of Robert Frost.* New York: Holt, Rinehart and Winston, 1969.)

<u>Alone Music</u>

Beethoven. *Moonlight Sonata*
Debussy. *Afternoon of a Faun*
Smetana. *The Moldau*
Sibelius. *In Memoriam*, op. 59
Tchaikovsky. *Overture to Romeo and Juliet*
Rachmaninoff. *The Isle of the Dead*, op. 29

Happiness

Sometimes happiness is not as easy to create as the so-called "negative" moods. Remember Brer Rabbit's Laughing Place, "take a frown, turn it upside down, and you'll find yours, I know-ho-ho." Children think differently about things that are funny. Talk with them about things and events that make them laugh or feel happy. Circus, monkeys, roller skating, football games, picnics, parties, dancing.

Sound effect records of people laughing can start children laughing. Let children demonstrate ways people laugh. Ask them, What does your body do when you laugh? Your eyes? Stomach? Legs? Try to differentiate between happiness and silliness. But silliness can make us laugh and laughing can make us happy. Studies have shown that laughter is good for us. Some people who are sick can get well by laughing a lot. People who laugh a lot don't get sick as often. Ask children why they think this is true, how they feel inside when they're laughing.

Read some happy poems. Play some funny or laughing music. Then have students write some similes about happiness, or complete the sentence, "I always laugh when...." or "I'm happiest when...." Writing can be prose or poetry or both.

"Happiness"

Happiness looks like a bright golden orange sun rising after a cool and refreshing rain followed by a beautiful rainbow with glowing colors. It smells as though you've gone outside for the first time. Happiness feels soft and squishy, yet hard and jagged at the edges. It has a loud yet warm and comfortable sound.

Kristi Archuleta
Age ten

Happiness is floating around on a pillow of air. Feelings of kindness wash over the body. The head soars above the rest of the people and nothing can be depressing. Even a cold winter day looks as if it will be a glorious one. Dark clouds evaporate and a new skin of blue sky is revealed. Winds cease to exist. Nothing can harm you.

Skip Wehner
Age fifteen

Happy Poems

Most limericks and nonsense poetry.
Carl Sandburg. "Happiness"

Stella Mead. "The Merry Man of Paris"
"The Funny Old Man and His Wife."
(Found in *Sung under the Silver Umbrella: Poems for Young Children*. New York: Macmillan and Company, 1956.)

James Whitcomb Riley. "The Lugubrious Whing-Whang"
(Wells, Carolyn. *A Nonsense Anthology*. New York: Dover, 1958.)

Happy Music

Debussy. Golliwog's Cakewalk, from Children's Corner Suite
Mendelssohn. *Spinning Song*
Offenbach. *Gaite Parisienne*
Piston. *The Incredible Flutist*
Saint-Saëns. *The Carnival of the Animals*
Strauss. *Till Eulenspiegel's Merry Pranks*
Tchaikovsky. *The Nutcracker Suite*

Fear

This emotion is fun to talk about and work with. It fits in nicely with the Halloween season and perhaps a unit on good horror writing. Children like to be scared by horror movies and Halloween spook houses. Movies and TV are so visual and so violent today that much of the first writing will reflect this. We feel that children need to get rid of this, but should be led on into good scary writing. One of the assignments we give is to write a horror story, but the one rule is no blood and guts, no real violence. Read from the works of Poe, LaFanu, Blackwood, Bleiler, Robert Chambers, and Shirley Jackson for mood pieces, ghost stories, which frighten but are not repulsive. Talk about the idea of something being more frightening when it is not seen, and the technique of the actual violence happening off stage. Talk about the kind of scared they get from ghost stories and movies versus a time when they were really frightened and didn't want to be.

Teacher: How do you feel when you're frightened? What does your stomach do? Your hands? Your face? Your mouth? Your throat? Now we're going to do something called The Silent Scream. Everyone stand. Something very scary has happened and you are going to scream as loudly and as hard as you can but no sound will come out. Ready? The scream starts at your toes. It goes up your legs. Your back and stomach tighten. It rolls up your chest, your throat. It sticks in your throat, tightening your eyes and scalp. All right. Relax and be seated. Write a piece of a story where the main character is frightened and screams. Remember how your body felt and write it in the story. Remember not to say, he's scared. Paint a picture of fear with words.

Share reading about the silent scream. See if children wrote vivid descriptions of how the body reacted. Would the reader feel the fear?

Creative Assignment

Show a picture of Edvard Munch's lithograph *The Cry*. Have children write what they feel after looking at the picture. Have children enter the picture and become the figure who is crying out, then write their feelings. Other works of Munch such as *Melancholy* and *Death Room* may be used in the same way.

Have children bring in passages from books they read where the characters are frightened. Share them with the class and discuss how the author wrote about fear. Did he make the reader afraid, shiver, look over his shoulder?

Activity

Set up this situation with a discussion or a mind trip. You go to visit a Haunted House, thinking it is a spook house put on by your friends. You get inside and find out it is real. Write about what happens.

Two records may be used along with this activity. Play either while the children write.

Chilling, Thrilling Sounds of the Haunted House. A Disneyland Record. DQ1257

Sounds to Make You Shiver. Pickwick Recordings. 135 Crossway Park Drive, Woodbury, N.Y. 11797.

An alternative activity to do with the Disney record is this. Side one sets up ten different situations with sound effects. Each of these could be a complete story with the sounds on the record as the climax scene. Children may each choose a different story or all may work on the same one. Writers often begin with the climax scene or the ending of a story and work backwards to plan the story. See how this technique works for the children.

Creative Assignment

Read Stephen King's short story, "The Lawnmower Man." Discuss the story. Assign the children to write a horror story about some household thing that comes alive and menaces him or his family.

Activity

Each child writes half a horror or mystery story. When he establishes the situation and gets his character in trouble, he stops and trades with someone in the class (by drawing names to be fair). The second person has to finish the story, getting the character out of trouble or into a satisfactory ending.

Activity

Musical writing chairs. In a group around a table each child starts writing a story. At the sound of a whistle pass papers to the right, give some time for reading and then keep writing. Change enough times so that story is back to original owner if possible. Give longer time for reading towards the end as the story gets longer. Read stories. This can be done with horror stories or any other genre. Obviously you may not get a great story with this game, but making writing fun is always a goal of any writing session. There is also a challenge here to think fast and take the plot forward quickly.

Scary Poems

Kathy McLaughlin. "Suicide Pond"
Donald Hall. "The Man in the Dead Machine"
(Found in *Some Haystacks Don't Even Have a Needle.* Edited by Stephen Dunning, Edward Lueders, and Hugh Smith. Glenview, Ill.: Scott Foresman, 1969.)

Maurice Sagoff. "Frankenstein by Mary W. Shelley"
Edward Field. "The Bride of Frankenstein"
Robert Siegel. "B Movie"
Ishmael Reed. "beware: do not read this poem"
(Found in *Pictures That Storm Inside My Head.* Edited by Richard Peck. New York: Avon, 1976.)

James Whitcomb Riley. "Little Orphant Annie"
(Many anthologies.)

Scary Music

Dukas. *The Sorcerer's Apprentice*
Mussorgsky. *Night on Bald Mountain*
Saint-Saëns. *Danse Macabre*
Wagner. *The Ride of the Valkyries*

Other Emotions

Explore other emotions such as anger, frustration, boredom, surprise, impatience, or conditions such as sleepiness, silence, heat, cold, luxury, richness, poverty, lethargy.

"Boredom"

Boredom. The domain where everything is quiet, white, and misty. Where there is no light, no color, nothing to do, just a feeling of emptiness and white mist going on endlessly. Never getting out until some color shows through the misty white, pulling you out. But boredom is like a clock ticking and ticking but never stopping.

Beth Sani
Age eleven

"Frustration"

Frustration is wanting to bite your aluminum bat when you strike out. It's when you can't find yourself in the scarlet anger you're experiencing. It smells hot, like a witch's brew with blood as the main ingredient. Frustration is not being able to make yourself function as you want to. It tightens the muscles of the face, the arms, and makes you want to smash anything that causes it. It's a terrible pain that lasts as long as you're angry, and dies away into a slow trickle.

Danny Reich
Age thirteen

USING MUSIC FOR MOTIVATION

In addition to using music for promoting emotional awareness, general classical music can be played and children asked to write their feelings prompted by the music. In doing this type of writing activity, first play the recording. Talk about the music. Then play it again while children write. Less imaginative children may get some ideas from the class discussion. Always suggest that each person will probably hear something different in the music. Tell the children, "Write down what *you* hear. What you see, the pictures in your mind as the music plays."

Other sound effect records may be used for stimulating writing, poetry or prose. A recording of crickets chirping or bees buzzing might kick off a writing period about insect orchestras. Electronic records might suggest outer space stories or enchanted forests and castles.

Good General Music for Writing Activities

Bernstein. *Fancy Free*
Copland. *El Salon Mexico*
Copland. "Hoe-down," from *Rodeo*
Copland. *Appalachian Spring*
Dvorak. *New World Symphony*
Gliere. *Russian Sailor's Dance*
Guarnieri. *Brazilian Dance*
Rossini. *William Tell Overture*
Stravinsky. *Firebird Suite*

USING PICTURES FOR MOTIVATION

Start a collection of pictures to use in your creative writing class, but also see if your public library or your school library has a picture file where you can check out pictures. Scenery, travel photos, pictures of faces, people doing things, children doing things, fine art—any of these may be used in various ways.

We use two methods of getting response to a picture.

Place Yourself in the Picture

Ask the children to step into the picture you either hold up, place in the overhead projector, or project onto a screen, and then wander around and write what they see and feel. Scenic pictures work well in this exercise. Exotic photos from other countries can stimulate the imagination. Futuristic pictures, fantasy, or abstract paintings will give a different type of writing. You might use many pictures to set a mood or experience. For instance, show picture after picture of fall foliage and then have them write about the changing of the season. Leave one picture on the screen and have all the children step into it and write about it. Each piece of writing will be different. Again point out to the class that all can use one idea and have different writing because of the experience the individual brings to the writing.

Creative Assignment

Have children draw abstract or surrealistic pictures with crayons or paint. They then can exchange pictures with another child, enter the picture, and write about the world they see there.

What Does the Picture Say to You?

Teacher: This picture cannot speak except through you.
You are the voice of the picture.
What does it say?

For best results with this method choose pictures where faces register emotion or where something is happening that suggests an emotion. A book called *The Family of Children* by Edward Steichen contains pictures of children from all over the world experiencing what all children know: joy, sadness, wonder, play, love, rejection, death. The book is softcover and we have had best results with unbinding the book in order to use the single pictures. Remind your writers that it's not necessary to start poems or prose with "this picture says." Jump right into what it says.

Using Pictures for Special Subjects

Collections of photographs can be used to coordinate with class studies or units. For instance, select pictures of animals who are endangered. Talk about endangered species, read and study about them. Then children enter the pictures to speak for them. Pictures about endangered species can be coordinated with the mind trips on endangered animals later in this chapter. Other photo unit ideas:

Historical events
Pioneers
Fantasy
Funny animal pictures
Underwater photos
Celebrations

CREATIVE DRAMATICS

Using drama to stimulate a child to write is successful, because some of the same thinking goes into writing about a character or pretending to be a character, writing a scene or acting as part of that scene. You can experience various emotions through acting out a character, then write down feelings that seemed real.

Mini-Scenes

Have one or more children walk across the room being old. Talk about how a body slows down when older, but that not all old people are the same.

Talk Session

Teacher:	Steve, would you walk across the room like you think an old person might walk? That's good. Class, how old do you think Steve is?
Lucy:	Eighty, at least. My grandmother is sixty, and she doesn't walk that way.
Teacher:	All old people are different, aren't they? I know a man who is eighty-one and still plays tennis. Another who is eighty tap dances.
Sarah:	My grandmother rides a motorcycle.
Teacher:	But a person's body does slow down, doesn't it? If you can run, you can't run as fast or as far.
Johnny:	My grandmother broke her arm running for a phone.
Teacher:	Yes, bones do break easily. And some minds grow older, but sometimes a person's body is old and his mind isn't. How would that feel?
Mary:	It would be awful to wish you could roller skate, but you have to sit in a rocking chair instead.
Teacher:	Let's pretend you are very, very old, at least eighty. Walk around the room being eighty. Then come back to sit in your chair still being very old. Write something on your paper about being very old.

"The Dark Is Near"

The dark is growing closer.
The dark is coming near: the very simple reason is that I am 89.
My spine is growing benter, my back is growing weak.
And when I move my legs I know it's coming near.
It's surely to be here by the time that I can hear
 crystal sounds inside my ear.

Ben and Dylan
Age twelve

Have children pretend to be people who are sad, lonely, any of the emotions, and then write down how they felt while they were those people. You can combine pictures and drama. Show a picture. Have children act or walk as they imagine the person in the photo would act or walk or talk.

Act Out a Full Story

It is easier to do the drama with a small group of children, but if you can involve children in a story quickly, they will stay in it. (Use all-purpose room for a full class.) The story that follows is made up, but you may use old tales or stories that would make good short dramas. We like to use a drama that is open-ended and then leave the ending to the children.

Talk Session

"The Strange Disappearance of Lucille"

Teacher: Let's gather in a circle and sit down. We are camping. Dinner is over. We've washed the dishes. It's a cool evening and we are enjoying a warm campfire. The fire crackles and snaps. Smell the wood smoke. (Give children time to react to a question or action.) I love a campfire. What shall we do? Did anyone bring a guitar? I know. We can sing songs or tell ghost stories.

Mary: Let's tell ghost stories. I know one, it's about....

Teacher: Wait a minute, Mary. Excuse me for interrupting you but Lucille isn't here. Has anyone seen Lucille?

Children: I haven't. She was here a minute ago. I haven't either.

Lucy: Maybe she went to the bathroom.

Teacher: Lucy, you and Mary go check the bathroom. John and Rebecca, look in all the tents.

Gary: Didn't she go to the stream to wash dishes?

Teacher: I'll look by the creek. The rest of you stay right here. (Everyone comes back.) No luck? Well, I hate to leave the fire, but we must look for her before it gets any darker. Let's bank the fire so it doesn't spread.

Steve: We'd better get a flashlight.

Teacher: Good idea. Take a partner and stay close together. (All start down path looking and calling out.) My, it's dark. Darn, my flashlight batteries must be old. My light is getting dim. So is yours, Steve.

Beverly: Mine too. (Others, me too.)

Teacher:	All the lights are going out. That's strange. Thank goodness for that sliver of moon. And it's coming out from behind the clouds. We can see a little. It will have to do. How do you feel being out in the woods at night?
Rebecca:	Scared. Maybe there are ghosts out here.
Sue:	I'm cold. Let's go back.
Teacher:	No one is going back until we find Lucille. And we must stay together. I don't want to lose anyone else. (Calls.) Lucille! Lucille! Listen. No, I don't hear a voice. What do you hear?
Gary:	An owl hooting.
Bill:	Branches snapping.
Susan:	A cricket. That's a friendly sound.
Teacher:	I could use some friendly sounds. Oops! The path is getting rocky. Be careful. Look! I didn't know there was an old house out here.
Children:	Me either. It looks spooky. I'm scared.
Teacher:	There's one light in that upstairs window. Maybe Lucille came too far, got lost, and would go to that house. Let's go see. What does the old house look like?
Children:	Spooky. Rotting. Falling down. A castle. A witch's house.
Teacher:	We'd better knock since someone seems to live here. (Knocks on door. Listens. Knocks again.) Look, the door is opening. How does the door sound? It hasn't been opened in a long time. Why, no one is there. Who opened it? I guess we have to go in. Sure is scary. Let's go upstairs, check the lighted room, and get out of here. I'm sure Lucille must be here. Watch out, there are cobwebs on the stairs. That step is broken! Don't fall. Look at this old picture. Here, that door has a sliver of light under it. You knock this time, Gary. Look! The door is slowly opening.

Now, everyone tiptoe back to your seats and write the rest of the story. You can start any place in it. You can change anything you like. Don't have too many characters. Make the reader feel he is there when he reads the story. Put in smells, feels, sights, noises. Tell how the characters feel.

Notice that the teacher steps out of the story occasionally to remind children to take part, to ask questions that stimulate their imagination. Another way is to stay in the story, pausing when you give a clue as to what is happening; and when you give directions for writing, talk about night sounds, feeling, and so on. Older children may try to trip you up—one boy made all the flashlights come back on. You will have to be creative enough to steer the story in the direction you want or to take it into a new direction if it sounds good and you feel comfortable with making it up as you go. The teacher needs to stay in control of the story, but leave the ending open so every child has the fun of saying what was behind the door. Having had the dramatic experience, the make believe of actually being there, the children will write good stories.

Other Creative Dramatics Suggestions

An Enchanted Forest: How does it look? How does it feel? Sounds? Smells? Keep the forest dark. A floating hand that shimmers with light beckons and you step into a clearing that is flooded with light. What do you see in the clearing? What happens to you there?

Down the Rabbit Hole: How does it feel to go down? How does it look? Leave what you find at the bottom of the hole or after walking a distance to the children's imagination.

On a Spaceship to Another Planet: Something goes wrong and you have to make an emergency landing. Step out of the ship and into an alien environment.

Inside a Coconut: (Or other fruit or vegetable.) We're walking in a jungle and come onto a giant coconut. (Or a small one and we shrink.) Slowly a small door opens and we go inside.

Through a Color Wheel: Each world you enter is one color. As the wheel turns slowly you are able to step through the shimmering blue, green, red, the color of your choice. The world beyond is all that color. What are the different words for the color you choose?

Red	Scarlet	Carmine	Cinnabar	Puce
Cinnamon	Pink	Wine	Fuchsia	Ruby
Brick	Coral	Burgundy	Maroon	Sienna
Rust	Cherry	Rose	Vermilion	Claret

This last drama provides a good opportunity to talk about using color in a scene. Red can make the reader feel warm; blue can create a feeling of cold. Talk about using color to create an emotion. Ask questions: If you are in a desert scene what color would predominate? A snowy scene? What if you wanted the reader to feel peaceful and relaxed? Describe a room decorated mainly with one color. What kind of person lives in this room? What is the favorite color of your main character?

Bring in a scene to share where an author uses color well. Discuss why he chose that color.

MIND TRIPS

Often it is not convenient to walk the class through an actual acting out of an experience. In this case you can do a mind trip. In this exercise the teacher instructs the children to get comfortable, close their eyes, go into themselves, and have an experience in their minds as he or she talks. Children do not talk. A teacher should pause as needed to give children time to get into the drama, the time to experience a situation as he or she talks.

Pet Rock

Sit down beside your desk taking up as little space as possible because you are very small. Close your eyes. Now you are a rock. How does it feel to be a rock? Where are you sitting? In a stream? Beside a stream? In the desert? On a mountain? What do you hear where you are sitting? You have been there a long, long time. One day someone comes along. He lifts you and puts you in his pocket or in a box or a bag. How do you feel now? What is around you? What sounds do you hear? What smells? Now he takes you somewhere else. Where is it? Is it a house? A store? Now you are on a shelf. What do you see, smell, hear? Maybe someone buys you. What if the person who picked you up got tired of you? He takes you off the shelf and throws you away. Where does he throw you? How do you feel? Is where you are better or worse? What happens next? Get back into your seat and write the Pet Rock story. You may change the story in any way.

While the creative dramatic experience is more often left open-ended, the mind trip can be a whole experience. Challenge the children to change your idea in any way they like. They can use it for a jumping-off place, the seed for their own stories. Praise the new ideas. (We find that young children like the pet rock story better than older children. But remember that it is all right to try things that don't work out well. And it is all right for some children not to like every thing you try. What is important is for a teacher to try a variety of techniques. A child will take what he likes best for his own mind trips or ways to turn himself on.)

Endangered Species

You are *hawk*. You are flying very high in a blue sky. Because your wings are not very strong, you ride the warm air currents. The thermals. Flap, flap, flap, you wing up to find the warm air. Then you glide round and round, higher and higher. Another hawk flies beside you now. This is your mate. Together you seem to float in the blue sky. Then you circle down, down, down, close to the earth, looking for a high tree on which to land and rest. Suddenly there is a noise. Zing, Ping. Your mate cries out and falls from the air beside you. Down, down, down, the injured hawk falls. Out of sight, and you are left alone — flying alone. Below two boys with guns laugh and walk on.

You are *wolf*. You sit by your den preparing for a hunt. You stretch and then howl on a long, eerie note. Another wolf joins in the song and soon all are howling. You love the music. Then trot, trot, you are off for the evening's hunt, getting food to bring home to the babies in your den. Your long legs stretch out as you lope along, putting your back feet in the track of your front. Cull-op. Cullop, Cullop. You set a slow steady pace that you could keep up all night. Suddenly overhead a terrible noise clacks and grinds. Closer and closer to the pack it comes. A funny bird with a whirling wing chases you until you are exhausted. Bang! A shot rings out and the old wolf running beside you, your mother, falls. You want to stop and help her but on and on the machine chases you and your family. Shot after shot rings out until you are the only wolf left. You drop exhausted in a clump of trees behind a bush.

You are *cheetah*. You live on an African savannah. The sun is warm and you can stretch your legs and run up to seventy miles an hour. Then you rest in the shade of a tree and watch three spotted babies at play. One day after a hunt, you lie under your tree chewing a bone when suddenly something flies over you. Swish! You try to leap up and run but you find you are trapped. You struggle, leap, and snarl, but you cannot break loose. Caught even tighter, you are loaded into the back of a truck. For a long time you bump over a dry, dusty road. Then you are placed in a cage and into the darkness for an even longer trip. You are thirsty and tired but you are afraid to sleep. Finally you are released and you try to run but there is no place to go. Wire walls stop you in every direction and creatures on two legs stare at you.

You are *killer whale*. You swim in a vast ocean with your mother and father and several other family members. When you are tired the water rocks you gently as you lie on the surface, floating and dozing. When you are playful you leap out of the water, swooshing back down, pushing waves into the air. Sometimes you rub against a female who is your friend or your mother. Her smooth skin feels good on yours. You jump over her, swim under, squealing and shrieking. One day a terrible noise makes you stand on your tail and look out over the water. A huge smelly thing is coming toward you. Your father signals to you to dive and he swims between you and the huge object. But when you surface to breathe something swishes over you and you are lifted from the water. The rope burns your sensitive skin. You are so frightened. You squeal and squeal. Your family gathers round you, calling out to you, but they cannot help. You are lifted high into the sky, out of the water, and placed on a hard surface. You continue to cry out and you can hear the voices of your father and mother. A loud noise makes the surface all around you vibrate, but you keep listening until you can no longer hear your family call to you.

The above mind trips on endangered species can be used one at a time. For instance, do the wolf piece and combine it with the Natural History Magazine recording of wolves howling and wolf information. Then the children write about wolves only. The same can hold for the killer whale and recordings of whale voices. You can use all the mind trips at one time, pausing between each, talking, and then letting the children select which animal they wish to write about. A good follow-up is to instruct the children to start a free-verse poem with "I am _____" pretending they are the animal and writing their experience.

The Language and Music of the Wolves. Natural History Magazine. New York, 1971. (Narrated by Robert Redford)

Songs of the Humpback Whale. Capitol Records, ST-620.

> *I am eagle.*
> *I roam the skies of Colorado.*
> *I hunt during the day.*
> *And return to my young when the sun sets.*
> *I bring home food of mice or rabbits.*
> *And soon young eagles will fly.*
>
> Andra
> Age nine

> *I am snow leopard.*
> *I run free and wild.*
> *My life is simple yet pleasant.*
> *Through the forest I run,*
> *leaping and sprinting.*
> *I run late at night*
> *when the world is still.*
>
> Karin Krauth
> Age twelve

> *I am tiger.*
> *I roam the jungle.*
> *I am king and I rule all*
> *beasts of the jungle.*
> *I live in a grassy area*
> *with many trees.*
> *I like it here because it is*
> *my habitat.*
>
> Beth Sani
> Age ten

(Poems continue on page 68.)

I am wild mustang.
I am endangered because
People catch me and tame me
>*so soon there will be tame mustangs,*
>*instead of wild ones.*
Here is my story.
One day my leader went ahead and never came back. We
mares were worried. A few days later another stallion came
and claimed our herd as his. He was big and swift. The
other was weak but swift. He led us to man and we were all
caught except for a handful. But one by one we're getting
caught, soon there were only three. One day we heard
thunder on the ground and we saw our leader leading
about fifty mares. Then he saw us and nudged us into the
herd. Up till now I was free and I will stay free.

Margie McIntosh
Age eight

I am wolf.
The pack is hungry.
The pack must eat.
The pack goes looking.
The pack finds meat.
Enemy bear is wanting our food.
We will not give him any.
He jumps on us.
We claw and tear.
He is dead, the pack lives.
His dead body will feed the pack.
But the pack is hungry.
The pack must eat.

John McIntosh
Age eleven

There were cold nights when he ran against the wind, and the icy
rain awoke him to a consciousness of the joy of life. There was the
hill-top meeting place where he sat with other wolves in the moonlight,
and howled his joys and sorrows and boasted of his mate and cubs.
There was the warm den where he lay to rest from a long day's work,
where he was safe and alone, and no one dared to intrude upon him.
There was the thrill of the chase, of the other wolves working with him
as one wolf.

Then suddenly, he was put in a place that had walls, that had
boundaries, that confined his spirit in a cage smaller than the hill-top.
There were creatures, creatures that he had never seen before, that
stared at him when he wished to be alone. He no longer had anything
to hunt, and his food was thrown to him in a dead, lifeless lump that
would not run when he chased it, and had none of the flavor of the

wild. There were other wolves, but they kept apart. There was no longer anything to tie them together, for the days were long and dull, and there was no purpose to his life anymore.

Diane McConkey
Age thirteen

NOTES

1. Mary Q. Steele. *Journey Outside* (New York: Viking Penguin Inc.), 61.

2. Steele, *Journey Outside*, 29.

six

Teaching Technique of Writing

Writing a complete story is like putting together a jigsaw puzzle.

Writing a complete story is like putting together a jigsaw puzzle. All the pieces must add up to a finished picture. They must fit together at the end. There must not be a piece missing. Neither should there be one left over. This is the challenge an author faces every time he starts a new story.

You can't teach anyone to write, but there are basic techniques that children can learn. These are the same techniques that we teach to adults or anyone who wants to improve his story telling.

Ways to teach technique include explanation, example, and having children write specific parts of a story. The techniques covered in this chapter are characterization, plot, viewpoint, beginnings, foreshadowing, transitions, emotion, description, action and suspense, black moment or crisis, climax and endings.

First, explain a technique to students, giving a reason for its use. Read students examples of the technique. We recommend using examples from great literature, current popular fiction from adult or children's books, and work of other students in the same age range as your class. Build up a file of childrens' work by getting permission to duplicate particularly good examples. Use examples in this book.

Have children write pieces of stories, working on different techniques. Children should not worry about technique as they write or stories will become mechanical. Most technique is learned by a sort of osmosis. But one has to write a great deal to have this happen. If you are playing a tennis match and think about how you hold your racquet, how you will hit the ball on every shot, you probably will not play well. The professional practices parts of a game before a match; during the match she plays intuitively. Writers also use technique intuitively after much practice. During the editing stage of writing, point out to the child how techniques were used well, or how something can be improved. Have the child rewrite pieces of a story to make them better.

CHARACTERIZATION

Characterization is the single most important element in a story. This is what makes the story come alive. If the characters seem real to the reader, the story will be real.

Is it important for children who are writing to work on in-depth characterization? We think it is. Writers are observers of people. Children are skilled at seeing people as they really are. We have all been with a child when he reads right through—or between the lines of—what an adult was saying.

Insight into character and personalities and understanding of what goes into people to make up their personalities help us to deal with people in our lives. The child who has written a character sketch of an elderly man or woman will have empathy with the problems of getting old. The student who writes a story about a person who is handicapped will be more tolerant and understanding of anyone who is different.

A WRITER IS A PEOPLE WATCHER

Encourage children to people watch. Writers deal with emotion. When writers see someone laugh, they say to themselves, what made that person laugh? When writers see someone cry, they look for what is behind the emotion. They think, how does that person feel? While looking at people around them they are always wondering, what is that person's life like? What would it be like to be him or her?

Creative Assignment

Assign an after school or weekend writing while people watching. Suggest that students take pencil and paper to their nearest mall or large shopping center. While there they observe people and write one-liners or short sketches of the people they see. Encourage their use of descriptive words, simile. Share these sketches in the classroom. Evaluate by saying, "can we see that person?"

> *She walked tall, swinging her ponytail behind her and overworking her hips which looked like a piece of machinery swinging back and forth.*
>
> Beth Sani

> *Leisurely he walked down the mall, holding his colorful creations in his grubby hand. He was dressed all in white as if to signify that only his creations were important. He looked as if he knew nothing, lost in space.*
>
> Beth Sani

A middle-aged woman, walking like ... well, like she was trying to lose weight. But she was carrying a coke in one hand and a box of popcorn in the other.

Greg Reich

A gum chewer with a walk like a peacock. He wears sunglasses, as if to hide a pair of cold, forbidding eyes.

Danny Reich

She has high-heel shoes and short curly hair. She has a short, dignified and purposeful walk, not unlike that of a schoolteacher.

Danny Reich

His hair flew out in all directions, grey to match his bushy eyebrows. He looked exactly like Beethoven and walked like he was only eighteen.

Heather Aker

Creative Assignment

Let children make posters for the writing room or corner using these rules for writing better characters:

Crawl inside a character.

A writer is a people watcher.

In a story there are round characters and flat characters.

The character is not a robot run by a writer.

A writer lives the story with the characters as it happens.

Writers need to know their characters as well as they know themselves or better. They will know their characters better than they know real people. The characters become real people in their minds. How do writers do this? They spend time thinking about a character before they write a story. Maybe their character writes them letters or notes. In a short story the main character will have one major character trait. But the writer will know much more about him. On page 76 is a character chart which can be duplicated for children to use in planning characters. Caution them not to use the chart to create a character, but to think about a character, who he is, what he's like. Then use the chart to finish rounding him out.

How Well Do You Know Your Character?

Story:

Character:

Author:

Date:

Character's sex: _____ Age _____ Height _____ Weight _____

Color Hair _____ Color eyes _____

How does your character look in general? (Neat, sloppy, little, big, like a grey wren, like a grouch, etc.)

People's first impression of him?

Where does your character live?

Does he/she like living there?

How many other members of the family are there? Who are they?

How does he/she get along with the family?

What does your character do for a living?

If in school, what grade?

What jobs has he/she had?

Does he/she like his/her job?

How does your character get along with other people?

Does he/she have any friends? Who are they?

How did/does your character feel about school?

Is he/she smart_____ slow_____ Quick to understand things_____ Slow to understand?

Is your character creative? In what ways?

What talents does your character have?

What is he/she most interested in doing?

What hobbies does he/she have?

Does your character have any superstitions? What are they? Where did they come from?

What is he/she afraid of?

What are his/her favorite books?

What are his/her favorite TV shows?

Favorite foods?   Snack foods?

What kind of clothing does he/she like to wear?

What are your first impressions of his/her personal appearance?

Can you make any comparisons of your character? (Like a machine, a grizzly bear, a kitten, a tornado, a dictionary, etc.)

How does he/she feel about:
Health?

Other people's opinions of him/her?

Adventures?

Learning new things?

God?

Himself/herself?

Is he/she most often happy? sad? scared? lonely? angry? Why?

If your character could have three wishes what would they be? Why?

What is your character's ambition in life?

How does your character feel about himself/herself:
At the beginning of the story?

At the end of the story?

What is your character's major character trait?

Does it or could it get him/her in any trouble?

Would he/she like to change it?

(Character chart continues on page 78.)

Circle any other traits this character has:

ambitious	energetic	neat	stupid
awkward	excitable	patient	stubborn
bitter	fanciful	poetic	sweet
brave	forgiving	proud	superstitious
boastful	gentle	practical	understanding
boring	hateful	quarrelsome	vain
careful	honest	romantic	wasteful
cheerful	imaginative	self-centered	wise
clever	intelligent	selfish	other
creative	kind	shy	_____
clumsy	lonely	sincere	_____
cowardly	loving	smug	_____
dignified	lazy	silly	_____
dishonest	loyal	sloppy	_____
dull	mean	stingy	_____

PLOT

Plot is a character with a problem and what he or she does about it. Answering these five questions will lead you to a complete story.

Who?   Your characters.

Where?

When?   Your setting.

What?   Your problem.

Why?   Your premise or theme, and motivation for story to happen.

A strong character trait is often the element that causes a character to have a problem. Help children brainstorm to get a plot using a character trait.

Talk Session

Teacher:	This character, let's call him Joe, is lonely. What problem could he have because he's lonely?
Child:	He might want a friend.
Child:	He might want a friend so bad he'd get the wrong kind.
Child:	Yeah, in the wrong crowd.
Teacher:	Maybe they let him in on the edge of the group.
Child:	He doesn't really belong.
Child:	Maybe he's new in town too.
Child:	And he doesn't know these guys are bad.
Teacher:	What could they want him to do that he knows is wrong? He'd have to choose between having them for friends or doing the wrong thing.
Child:	Shoplifting.
Child:	TP-ing someone's house.
Teacher:	Isn't it okay to TP someone's house? Doesn't that say you like the person?
Child:	Yes, but they don't like this person, and they're doing it to annoy him.
Child:	And he calls the police.
Teacher:	All right. You write the story up to there and then decide what Joe does. You can give him other character traits or things he can do well. You can also give him a family.
Child:	Maybe he doesn't have a real family either.
Teacher:	Good. You decide what else he is like.

Always share the writing of the children — those who want to share. Children learn from each other. They take pride in sharing something good. Frequently a quiet child will have a very sensitive story or put beautiful thoughts on paper. Writing is often a haven for some children, those who may have no other area in which they excel.

Activity

Children create a character using the character chart or in a writing session through creative dramatics or a mind trip. (See chapter on special effects.) In the next session the teacher devises the situation. Each child writes a story or a scene in which his character reacts. Each story will be different because each character is different. Share these stories and point out how the different characters change the scene dramatically. Here are some suggested situations:

Trapped in an elevator

Working in a tennis ball factory

Present during a robbery

In a sinking ship

Victim of a practical joke

Winner in a contest or TV show

Lost in the desert

On the first public transportation to the moon

Touring the museum of modern art

In an old house on a stormy night

At the Queen's tea party

A variation on this activity is for each child to choose a well-known character such as Superman, Alice in Wonderland, Scrooge, movie or TV star. How would this person, whose character is established, act in one of the above situations?

TV character, Daryl, at the Queen's Tea Party: As Daryl enters the Queen's plush living room he struts, knowing that he is cleaner than he ever has been before. He just shaved his back and patched up the holes on his smelly tee-shirt. As the Queen extends her hand to shake his, he conspicuously spits on his own so that everyone will know it is clean. Unfortunately the Queen faints so that he never gets a chance to shake her hand.

After reviving the Queen by sticking his armpit up to her nose, they both sit down for a cup of tea. To check to make sure it is not too hot, Daryl pokes his ring finger in his cup before slurping up the tea. Next comes the cakes. Daryl once more spits on his hands to clean them before taking a handful of cake. After devouring his portion, Daryl once more cleans his hands, because it's polite, by wiping them on the red satin couch. For some strange reason Daryl was never invited to the Queen's house again.

Matt Jolley
Age fourteen

Activity

Choose a partner. One child writes a character sketch. The second describes the problem/situation. After these are written in detail, children trade character and plot. Each child writes a complete story, using the combined character and plot outlines.

Whether character or plot comes to mind first is the old chicken and egg argument. In reality, sometimes one comes first, sometimes the other.

Have children take a plot and brainstorm for the character.

Talk Session

Teacher:	A boatload of people is going scuba diving. One diver gets in trouble. Who can help save him?
Child:	There is someone on the boat who can do it.
Child:	Only one person. Make it hard.
Teacher:	Maybe he's not one of the people diving.
Child:	Maybe no one knows he can dive.
Teacher:	Why doesn't anyone know? Has he kept it secret?
Child:	Maybe he's a famous diver and is in disguise.
Teacher:	Why has he done that?
Child:	Maybe he got in trouble the last time he dived.
Child:	He almost died.
Child:	And now he's never going to dive again.
Teacher:	Maybe he's scared. Can people who are good at something get scared of it?
Child:	Sure. My daddy fell last time he went climbing and he says he won't go again. It was a close call.
Teacher:	So the "secret diver" is our main character? We have to know what happened to make him scared even if it won't be in the story.

Now it is time to do a character chart of the main character. Or even brainstorm what he is like before writing. We have a character, a problem; what he does about it is the story. There are other elements to discover: his age, male or female. How someone discovers he can dive. What makes him come forward. How he feels is important. Leave these details to the writer and again you will have thirty different stories.

Many writers work out the whole plot before they start writing. Others have some idea of what will happen, but start writing to discover the rest. How much of the plot to work out beforehand depends on personal preference.

VIEWPOINT

Viewpoint in a story is simply a matter of deciding how the story is told and whose story it is. Simplify viewpoint for children by suggesting that there is a camera inside the viewpoint character. In first person the camera is inside the main character. There is a picture of only what the main character can see, feel, or deduct. *I* can see what is happening. *I* can feel my reactions. The *I* character can guess how another character feels by the way that character acts or by what he or she says. In most first person narrative stories the focus is on the person telling the story. There is also the story in which the *I* character tells the story, but the focus of the camera is on another person, the main character. "I can't remember exactly when I realized that John was afraid. But it probably had something to do with our last trip."

In third person the camera is inside the author but focused on the main character. The author writes only of what the main character can see, feel, and deduct, but we are looking at the character move about in his or her environment. "Sarah skipped out to the mail box. Surely there'll be a letter, she thought. They've been gone a week. The air was cold and she pulled her sweater tightly round her shoulders."

In omniscient viewpoint stories the camera is placed at a distance from a scene so that we see everything, one whole, big picture; but it can also focus on one individual or one small part of the scene. We know all that is happening, inside everyone's head. It is best, though, when written so scenes aren't jumpy, and the focus doesn't change from person to person in one scene. When the focus shifts, or we go into another character's head, the scene changes.

"Shipwreck"

First Person: Salt water stung in my eyes. I gasped. Quickly I tried to grab hold of a salt-smelling beam which had been washed off my father's boat. Using all the strength I had, I fought the battle of ocean waves and grabbed onto the beam. Exhausted, I lay limp on the log which was being tossed about wildly.

Third Person: She heard her father yell. "Abandon Ship!" Off she went into the daring waters. A mouthful of water ran around her mouth, leaving a yucky aftertaste. Quickly she tried to swim toward the not-quite waterlogged beam.

Omniscient: The boat suddenly bashed against an iceberg, leaving a huge hole in the front of the ship. Ocean water quickly poured in as if it had been waiting for this moment all along. The crew's panic-struck faces were filled with fright. The ship was sinking. Sally's father, who had just seen the whole thing, quickly thought of his daughter, who had never learned to swim.

Jacey Tramutt
Age eleven

(Notice how in the omniscient scene, Jacey had the camera at a distance, filming the large scene, then moved it in closer and closer until we got to the father. I found she did this instinctively.)

"The Dragon"

First Person: "Help," I screamed as I felt the giant claw grab me and lift me up into the air. I saw the giant gnashing teeth getting close. I screamed again, but I thought, this is the end. I was still moving upward. Suddenly I felt myself being hurled against something wet and squishy. I looked up and saw a huge wall of white coming straight at me. I screamed in fear. Then again in pain as I felt something sharp jabbing through my chest....

Third Person: The arm of the beast lifted him high into the air, hurtling him into its mouth, still screaming as he died.

Omniscient: The huge dragon lifted the terrified villager high, as with its other claw it grabbed a horse. It shot a stream of fire into the stockade walls. It then threw the man into its mouth, bit once, then swallowed. He gulped the horse in two bites. Its tail started thrashing wildly, knocking down houses. Then it took to the sky to survey the damage it had done.

Jeff Hunt
Age thirteen

BEGINNINGS

Beginning a story is difficult for some children. The beginning of a story should introduce the main character and the problem. Most important, it should set the mood.

There are five types of beginnings that children can use:

1. Action
2. Situation or problem
3. Character
4. Dialogue
5. Setting or mood

Select beginnings from stories or books to illustrate these types and read aloud. Let children identify the type of beginning. Do not hesitate to use adult literature. Sometimes the types of beginnings will be mixed.

Let children practice writing beginnings. Some children tend to use the first paragraph to introduce themselves.

"Hi. I'm Carrie and I'm going to tell you this story about what happened to me on the way to school yesterday. I'm eight years old and in the third grade. Well, here's the way it happened."

Then usually the story starts in the second paragraph. Sometimes we aren't sure where a story starts. Suggest that students start anywhere and come back later and rewrite. Good beginnings are more often rewritten than written, so tell children to jump right into their stories.

<u>Sample Beginnings</u>

*Bob decided if the teacher gave them one more crazy assignment he
would flunk rather than do it. He was in enough trouble from last
week's assignment.*

*Stealing was wrong. Marcia knew that, and if she had to shoplift to
get into Lucy Leonard's club, she'd rather not have any friends.*

*The wolf was old and all alone. He must find a meal soon or he would
die.*

*I was so scared. This was my first deep-space assignment and I knew I
had to prove myself. But so soon? To make matters worse everything I
had ever learned seemed to have disappeared.*

*"Hello, Skylar? This is Ben Wearing. I've had the package delivered to
your address. But whatever you do, don't open it until I get there."*
*"Good thing you called, Ben. I had the scissors in my hand. How long
till you arrive? And why all this mystery?"*

*The old house crouched on a hill. Spanish moss dripped from near-by
trees like tendrils of hair. The house peered through the moss as I
approached, stumbling on a broken slate in the walk.*

*Five hundred balloons lifted off and floated toward the blue sky. The
celebration was just starting, and I hurried so as not to miss anything.*

Think of the beginning of a story as a shop window. Readers should look in
the window and want to come in. Remember, too, if they look in the window and
see toys, they don't want to come in and find it's a clothing store. Whatever
figures in the climax or end of a story should be introduced in the beginning. If
magic is in the story, it should be there at the beginning. The main character
should have the first line and already be in a situation or getting into it.

Another way to think of a beginning is as a fish hook with a tempting worm.
The reader is a hungry fish. The beginning should hook the reader and never let
him go. Have your writers look at their beginning as you ask these questions:
Would you read on? Have you used some magic words to tempt the reader? Have
you teased him? Made him curious?

A beginning is several paragraphs long, perhaps a fourth of the story. But
the first sentence must reach out and grab the reader.

FORESHADOWING

Foreshadowing is the promise of something to come: danger, fear, surprise,
trouble. The technique is used to plant clues so the story rings true at the end, and
so the reader isn't tricked or doesn't feel cheated because he didn't have all the
information he needed. It is used to enhance suspense and enjoyment of the
story.

We love thinking our main character is going to get in trouble. "I'm not going to get in any trouble," says Stanleigh, the raccoon, as he sneaks out of the house before his people get up. Now we know he is. We wiggle with anticipation. In a story where a bully is introduced we can hardly wait to see him get his comeuppance. We like the challenge of trying to solve a mystery before the main character does. All the clues must be there, skillfully hidden. We must be able to go back, reread, and say, yes, there it was. I should have known.

Foreshadowing is the showing of props used in a story. If the story problem is going to be resolved by use of a magic wand, the reader must see that wand in the beginning. The main character can't just pull a rabbit from a hat, a key from his pocket at the end and say, "Oh, yes, I forgot I had this."

In a story one of our students wrote the main character uses a ring to get rid of the threatening beast at the end. But nowhere before had we seen the ring. We suggested the character twist it on her finger early in the story as she stares out the window.

Sometimes just the way something is written is foreshadowing or the author will out and out tell us someone is different.

I knew there was something strange about my sister as soon as she came home from the hospital with mom. For one thing, she never cried. Never. She looked around the room a lot with questioning eyes never missing what was going on. And by the look in her eyes, it was almost as if she understood what was going on.

> Jacey Tramutt
> Age eleven

When we read this we know something strange is going to happen because the child is strange. (And strange is a magic word.)

Talk about planting clues for the reader. Have children bring in examples of foreshadowing from books they read.

TRANSITIONS

Transitions are bridges from one scene to another. We don't want to be reading a story set on a farm and suddenly find we're in the city. A scene or a sentence has to get us from one place to another.

Perhaps Sara is at home and we need to get her to the store to witness a robbery. A paragraph or so may be needed to get her there:

Sara turned off the TV set reluctantly. Go to the store? Dull, dull, dull. Nothing ever happened to her. At least on TV something happened. She kicked a rock as she walked the three blocks to the Saveway. Dull, dull, dull, her feet pounded out the rhythm. My life is dull.

As well as getting her to the store, we advance the story by foreshadowing. The reader suspects something is going to happen at the store this time. (And it had better happen; otherwise why make such a big deal about going?) Sara's life will cease to be dull in the next scene.

In another story, Phil and Mary plan a camping trip a week away. We don't want to go through that week because nothing happens. One sentence forms the bridge to get us to the next scene.

Mary thought the week would never pass, but finally on Saturday morning they loaded their packs in the car.

Inexperienced writers may think they have to take us through every scene and in this way they lose the tightness of a good story; the story rambles.

Every part of a story should advance it towards the end. If on the way camping, Phil and Mary stop to see Aunt Ruby, but the visit has nothing to do with the story, leave it out, or edit it out later. As readers we want only the good scenes, the action scenes, the scenes that heighten emotion, suspense, keep the story moving. Bridge the gaps between these scenes with strong transitions.

EMOTION IN WRITING

A story is always better if it touches the heart of the reader. You remember a story that makes you laugh or cry—one that sends shivers up your spine, keeps you on the edge of your chair. Showing how the main character feels is high on the list of things to do to make a story great instead of just okay. Notice we say showing and not telling.

Telling: Johnny felt bad when he made the last out.
Showing: Johnny swung. "Strike three," the umpire yelled, pointing towards the dugout as if that was where Johnny belonged. Johnny ducked his head, shuffled back towards his team, not daring to look anyone in the eye. He plopped on the bench and leaned his head on his hands.

Telling: Now that Gretchen had left, Mary felt lonely a lot.
Showing: Mary flopped on her bed, Gretchen's letter in her hand. She had thought she'd enjoy having the room to herself, but now Gretchen's side reminded her of being in a school after everyone has gone home.

Discuss the different types of emotion. See chapter 5 on special effects for more ways to teach children awareness of emotion.

Activity

Let children clip a picture of a person from a magazine and bring the picture to class. If possible it should be a picture of a person expressing some emotion. Talk about the picture.

Talk Session

Teacher:	(Holding up picture of boy with tears rolling down cheeks.) How does this boy feel?
Child:	Awful. He hurts inside.
Teacher:	How else do you feel inside when you are sad?
Child:	About to pop. My chest aches and there's a lump in my throat.
Teacher:	What does the lump feel like?
Child:	Like I swallowed a lemon.
Child:	My breakfast is right here.
Child:	A big hand is squeezing my throat.
Child:	My heart hurts till the tears can pop out.
Teacher:	After the tears pop out, do you feel better?
Child:	Sometimes. Sometimes I'm tired.
Child:	My eyes feel all washed away.
Teacher:	Why is this boy about to cry?
Child:	His dog got run over.
Child:	His mother died.
Child:	His father says he is moving to another house.
Child:	Someone told him he couldn't play.
Child:	He lost his lunch money.
Teacher:	How does your body feel when you're sad?
Child:	Hunched over. Droopy.
Child:	I want to curl in a ball when I'm sad.
Teacher:	Why do you want to curl into a ball?
Child:	So no one can get in.
Child:	I feel heavy when I'm sad.
Teacher:	How heavy do you feel?
Child:	As heavy as a sack of potatoes.
Child:	As heavy as a wet sleeping bag.
Teacher:	If a story started, "Tony felt as heavy as a wet sleeping bag," would you want to read it?
Child:	Yeah, I'd want to see why Tony felt that way.
Teacher:	On your paper describe someone who feels sad. Don't just tell us he feels sad. Show us a picture of sad. Heavy as a wet sleeping bag is a picture of sad. Hunched in a ball is a picture of sad. Write several lines as if this was a piece of a story.

"Hiding"

Hiding in your shell
When others are around.
Weeping within,
Bringing forth no sound.

Kiersten Remmers
Age thirteen

Excerpt from "Be a Friend to Get a Friend"

Most people don't know what it feels like to be lonely. But I do. It's like being outside in a freezing cold wind. You look around for someone, anyone to talk to or play with, only feeling the harsh wind nipping at your body. It's a bad feeling to have. I have it all the time.

Jacey Tramutt
Age eleven

Talk Session

Teacher: (Holds up picture of girl laughing.) How does this girl feel?
Child: Happy. She just got a birthday present.
Child: It was a puppy.
Teacher: How does her body feel?
Child: Like jumping up and down.
Child: Like it's full of air and could float.
Child: Wiggly.
Teacher: As wiggly as a new puppy.
Child: As wiggly as a rabbit's nose.
Teacher: When else would you feel wiggly?
Child: When you're excited.
Child: Sometimes I'm excited-scared, and I don't feel wiggly. Like when I'm getting on a roller coaster or going into a haunted house.
Teacher: So two emotions can overlap inside you or your character?
Child: Sure. You could be happy-scared if your daddy was coming home and you hadn't seen him for a long time.
Child: Sometimes I'm just smiley-happy, not wiggly-happy.
Teacher: Good. Write something about this girl or someone else who is happy. Don't tell us she's happy. Show us how she acts and feels and let us think, "Why, she's happy, isn't she?" Paint a picture of happy with your words.

Share pictures of people expressing dreamy, tired, angry, and have children discuss them and then write short descriptions of characters expressing those states. Don't try to do more than one or two characters at one session.

Activity

Have one child walk across the room and show an emotion. Let other children say or write how he was feeling or how he walked. Have entire class stand and as you talk about an emotion have each child make his body feel it. Give the children time to think before they react and then write down something about a character who feels that way.

Teacher: Something has happened to you. (Pause) Your body feels heavy. (Pause) A black cloud is pressing down on you. Your throat feels tight. Your eyes ache. A steel band around your head is getting tighter. It feels as if something is sitting on your chest. What are your hands doing? Sit down and write two or more lines about who you are, how you feel, and why you feel that way.

Teacher: You are sitting in a tree. (Pause) You lean back on a limb. (Pause) The sun is warm on your back. Your muscles relax. All the tightness inside you drifts away. Your mind goes out walking. It sees pictures as it walks. A gull floats on a stream of air. A porpoise dives slowly up and down in the water. He swims in a circle. Then he floats, letting the water wash over him. An otter floats on her back with her baby sitting on her chest. A mother cat licks her kitten. A bird preens his feathers. Sit down and write two or three lines about who you are, how you feel, and why you feel that way.

Creative Assignment

Write a description of a character doing something. Don't tell how he feels. Show us. Paint a picture with words. Let the class guess what your character is doing.

Larry pushed open the door. Leaning down he stepped out. His hair brushed his face, tickling his nose. His eyes squinted. He put out one hand and pressed forward, walking with difficulty. His coat flew open and he grabbed it, wrapping it round him. He pulled his lips tightly over his teeth, yet his mouth felt gritty. What is he doing? (walking in a strong wind.)

A WRITER FEELS HIS STORY HAPPEN.

Creative Assignment

Children bring pictures they've found at home that show a face with emotion. Each writes a paragraph or two about how the person in the picture feels. You may also trade pictures and write other paragraphs. Hang the pictures around the classroom with the writing or share them in some way.

Awareness is a big part of being a writer. Being aware of how people feel. Being tuned in to the human condition. Writing will make children more sensitive to people. These writing and sharing experiences will give teachers opportunities to be more sensitive to their students. One of our best writers wrote only of death, war, holocaust. When you see some repetition on subjects such as this, it is time for a private talk session between student and teacher: "Johnny, I see that you write most of your pieces about death and war. Do these things concern you? Would you like to talk about it? What other things interest you?" It is a privilege to be invited into a child's mind. Treat the experience in this way. All writers' egos are easily damaged, whether they be adult or child. Let each writing session build trust.

WRITING COLORFUL DESCRIPTION

The biggest weakness we have found in children's writing is that they *tell* the story rather than *show* it. This is true of emotion. It is also true of description.

Telling: Bill's desk was messy.
Showing: *The desk had paper scattered like seeds in a wind, pencils hanging over the edge of the desk like they were eavesdropping, and erasers in groups like mushrooms.*

Greg Reich
Age ten

Probably the best way to get across the idea of telling instead of showing is to read good writing, good examples of description. Stress painting pictures with words, using good verbs, descriptive words, similes, and metaphors. Stress using the right word. Praise good descriptive writing. Encourage children's observing, looking for detail, using the senses. (See chapter 5.)

Creative Assignment

Ask children to observe one room in their houses, preferably the messiest one or the one most lived in. Have them write down a description, bring it to class and share it. Did the writer show instead of telling? Can you see the room in your mind as the piece is read?

"Description of My Living Room"

My brother lying around like a Bahamas Beach Bum. His trombone case opened like a baby bird waiting to be fed. The television set like an eye waiting to open at any interesting thing. The stove in the fireplace looks like a square insect with handles as antennas and damper as fangs. The sofa looks like a very comfortable coffin and the stereo cabinet like a five-story doll house.

Greg Reich
Age ten

Observing the details in our environment is a skill that writers need to cultivate. Writing down those details puts the reader on the scene. Certainly we don't want pages of description and detail that slow the story. But we do want the scenes to come alive. Mix action with your description to keep it from slowing unless you need to slow a story down. Then a few lines of good description will aid suspense.

Creative Assignment

Read passages from literature to give children the idea of creating a sense of place. Then have them think of a place, and write a paragraph to make readers feel they are there. Criticize with this in mind. Do we feel we are there?

The bitter cold wind whipped the dull red dust through the air. The tall cliffs rose high above the deep valleys as the white of the frozen methane glittered in light from a distant sun. Two tiny moons floated across the sky, while on the horizon the tallest mountain in the solar system looked like an ant hill. The bright stars of earth and the moon shone in the sky. The air of the space suit had a strange scent to it. The water tasted metallic. The food rehydrated. The sun began to set over the western sky.

> Jeff Hunt
> Age thirteen

At night the school was almost pitch black. The only noise was the everlasting hum of the air-conditioner. The school smelled kinda like a new car. The chairs and desks made frightening black shadows on the floor and wall.

> Marc Wallace
> Age twelve

Assign a place for the whole class to describe. Read the descriptions aloud for illustrations of different ways to describe the same place. You could choose best lines for a class description.

A Museum of Natural History at Night: The museum had a very dim light. It cast strange shadows on the wall. The only sounds were the constant droning of the air-conditioning and the quiet ticking of the clocks. It smelled like a mopped floor. There was also a kind of musty smell like you could smell the age of the bones. The floor was slippery and wet. The air was chilly and dry. The air even tasted dry. Then the moon went behind a cloud and it turned blacker than black and the noises became louder until the moon came back.

> Marc Wallace
> Age twelve

A Yo-Yo Factory: As I walked in, my first impression was that of a coin mint. It smelled grotesquely synthetic, as if they were making nothing. As if the machines were molding nothing. Just working and making a foul smelling friction. I heard the machines purring like a cat with a bellyache except more regularly.

> Danny Reich
> Age thirteen

Sara went into the room. She heard sounds of machinery. Colors dazzling, pink, orange, green, blue, all of them vibrantly fluorescent. She smelled metal and fresh paint, and a slight smell of plastic. The machinery was constantly moving like an amusement park when you're on the ferris wheel looking down at the rides all moving in different directions, but somehow all connected.

Caitlin McDonnell
Age twelve

Suggestions for more places to describe:

Inside a cave

A fruit cellar

An underwater palace

Inside an ant hill

Big Foot's living room

Inside a whale's stomach

Inside an igloo

In an abandoned carnival grounds

Inside a school at night

In a mannequin factory

Inside a wolf den

In a hot air balloon surrounded by clouds

Inside an ice palace

In a giant's pocket

On an unknown planet

Description also helps us learn about someone's character. If we say someone drove a car, we know little about the character. But if we say someone drove a Corvette, we know he has money and has a flashy style. If the character drives a scratched and rusty '58 Chevy, we know he probably saved and bought it himself, and probably can work on it, so he is mechanical too. The way a person dresses helps to characterize, as does the way he keeps his room. Continue to remind student writers that they are painting pictures in a reader's mind. If they write, "a bird sang outside my window," the picture is vague and uncolorful. If they write, "a blue jay called out *helio, helio, helio*" we can see and hear the bird and we feel we are there in the scene.

ACTION AND SUSPENSE

Every good story has suspense — even stories that are not adventure or action or mystery. What will happen next? Will the main character solve his problem? Will he get out of the mess he's in? How will he do it? It is suspense that keeps us turning the page in any story. If we can put it down the writer has rambled, gotten off track, or not been skillful enough to keep us from figuring out what is going to happen. A story must not be predictable. Encourage children not to settle for the easy solution for any problem. Brainstorm for complications, other paths a story could follow and still be believable.

When you want a story to be very suspenseful or alive with action there are four ways to heighten the writing:

1. Step up the action.
2. Use action verbs.
3. Use short sentences or phrases.
4. Show how the main character feels.

BLACK MOMENT

Near the end of the story the situation gets so bad it looks as if the main character won't get out of his mess or solve his problem. This is called the Black Moment, or Crisis. Everything looks hopeless. The main character seems helpless. Now the rest of the story can be stated in a two-part question: Will Bill be able to solve his problem or won't he? Will Mary get the money to buy the horse she wants or will she have to keep riding the old nag at the stable? Will Hansel and Gretel be able to get out of the trap the witch has set for them and get back home or will they perish in the woods?

Let children point out the Black Moment in stories they read. Have them state the crisis in a two-part question. Have them check to see if their stories have a Black Moment. This is where the story pauses dramatically before it heads downhill for the climax scene and the ending.

CLIMAX AND ENDING

Where does a story end? For some children it's at the bottom of a page. They see the page ending and think, I have four lines to get to the end of the story. For some this is fatigue, so remind children they don't have to finish a story in one sitting.

(Jason and Rich are exploring a cave when they find a hidden room. Four men are talking about a bank robbery they have committed.)

Jason started to talk but Rich punched him and told him to be quiet. One of the men said, "If anybody finds our secret we'll punch him in the nose." Another man said, "We'll slit his throat." Another man said, "We'll tie him up and sit on him." Another man said, "We'd better look around and be sure no one is here." Rich and Jason were

*scared. They were scared that the men would discover them. So they
went outside and called the police.*

Jeff
Age ten

A story should end when the problem is solved. Certainly the problem was
solved when they called the police, and by calling them. But where is the
wonderful climax scene (the last big scene) that the reader has been waiting for,
has been led to expect? The reader feels cheated.

There are two possible endings to every story. The main character will solve
his problem or he won't. He will get out of the situation or he won't. He will get
what he wants or he won't get it. (He might get something better or discover that
he really didn't want what he thought he wanted, but this is all right. The reader
will be satisfied if the main character is.)

The story should build so that both endings seem possible right up to the very
end. The reader should never be sure just how the story will end. And the end
should satisfy the reader. Quite often children will build some wild fantasy story,
get the main character in a ton of trouble, then say, "Oh, it was just a dream."
The main character wakes up. This is not fair to the reader. He has gotten
involved in the fantasy and wants the main character to get out of the situation by
himself, his wits, his ingenuity, not some trick, or not get out at all.

The main character should always solve his problem himself. To have a
grown-up or another character come along and solve it for him isn't satisfying to
the reader either. If the writer has painted himself into a corner, as sometimes
even adult writers do, he can brainstorm all the possible ways the story could end,
all the things that are logical for the main character to do, all the things the writer
has planted that the character can do, his skills, his knowledge, his personality, or
a prop he might have that will do the trick.

All loose ends should be tied up in that final page or chapter. If you got a
horse in a ditch back on page one or left Mother tied up in the kitchen on page
four, you have to solve those problems too.

Remember that the main character has the first lines in a story so we know
whom to identify with. Now that same main character has the last lines. He may
say something, do something, think or feel some way. But it is his story, and we
want to know about him as the story finishes.

Remember Heather's story about the blue and yellow people? Look at how
the end of her story comes back to the beginning and uses that lovely symbol of
the clear teardrop. (And of course she commits suicide, in true Romeo and Juliet
fashion.)

*I stepped on the hall-walk leading out of the house and then
stepped on a sidewalk leading farther north than any other sidewalk. I
got off where it went into the ground and walked to the cliff. I looked
down, took a deep breath, and jumped. I then felt a wonderful, yet
terrifying sensation.*
   I was falling, falling.
   Like a teardrop.

Heather Aker
Age twelve

Lots of things to remember for just one story? Yes, but each is important. It will take time to learn all the techniques, to learn to use them well, but to do anything right you have to assemble all the tools needed for the job. These are the writer's tools and children can learn to use them. Not only will these techniques improve their own writing, but they will enjoy seeing those pieces of a story in the fiction that they read.

seven

Words, Words, Words

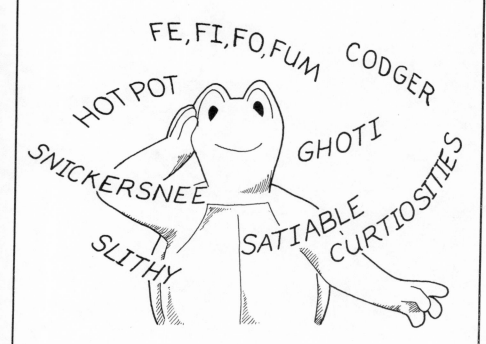

FE, FI, FO, FUM

CODGER

HOT POT

GHOTI

SNICKERSNEE

CURTIOSITIES

SLITHY

SATIABLE

"When I make a word do a lot of work,"
Humpty Dumpty told Alice, "I always
pay it extra."

> Words, in a world of wonders, are among the most wonderful adaptations of man. They are a complex music of meaning played upon himself as the orchestra. He is at once the performer and the instruments.
>
> Isaac Goldberg,
> *The Biology of Words*

Words are the tools of writers, the tools they use to give form and shape to the medium in which they work — ideas. As with any craftsman, writers keep their tools sharp and in good repair. They add new tools when they need them. They find new ways to use their old tools. We have said before that each person is unique and, therefore, can see and experience in a way in which no other person can. To share these unique observations we need words. The larger our vocabulary of figurative, descriptive words and phrases, the more vividly and accurately we'll be able to express our experiences.

So, obviously, if our children are going to make something of their ideas we must give them a vocabulary to work with. From the time children begin to talk we can encourage them to find pleasure in words — long words, short words, descriptive words, strange-sounding words. Rudyard Kipling knew that children like words, multisyllabic, alliterative, rhythmical, *difficult* words. Remember the Elephant's Child, full of 'satiable curtiosities, who lived by the great, grey-green, greasy Limpopo River at the time of the Precession of the Equinoxes?

Frank Lloyd Wright has written that he first became interested in architecture when, as a boy, he read the description of the great cathedral in Victor Hugo's *Notre Dame de Paris*.

> I was fourteen years old when this usually expurgated chapter in *Notre Dame* profoundly affected my sense of the art I was born to live with — lifelong: architecture. His story of the tragic decline of the great mother-art never left my mind.[1]

What if someone had told the young Frank Lloyd Wright, "Oh, that's too long and hard for you to read. All those dull passages that have nothing to do with the action. Here, take this comic book version called *The Terror of the Hunchback*. You'll like it better."

To oversimplify language, to make it too easy, deprives readers of finding fascinating new words, of enlarging their working vocabularies, and of discovering perceptive descriptions that only the right words, the perfect metaphors, can give.

From Psalm 147 we have two translations,

The Living Bible: *He sends the snow in all its lovely whiteness.*

King James Version: *He giveth snow like wool.*

Dorothy Grant Hennings and Barbara M. Grant, in their *Content and Craft*, write,

It is in the context of meaningful experience that vocabulary grows. Talking about the experience is the bridge to that vocabulary development.[2]

We can help our children learn new words. We can teach them to be brave enough to use new words. We can paraphrase Robert Browning and ask, "One's reach should exceed one's grasp, or what's an *experience* for?"

"We're not supposed to swim in the river any more," the small girl said. "It's condemned. No--" She frowned, struggling for the word she wanted. "No, I mean it is <u>contaminated</u>." "Yes," the librarian said, nodding. "I believe that is the better word."

WORDS

Word Collections

"Nothing frees the spirit like experience and the vocabulary to express it," Mauree Applegate writes.[3] So how are we going to build vocabularies that will free spirits and expression? Let's start with word collections. Young children can keep lists of words with sounds they like, of new words that they like to use. They can classify their words

happy words
funny words
scary words
noisy words
quiet words

Older children can add synonyms to these lists, observing the shades of difference in meanings, as in these synonyms for *quiet* and *afraid*:

hushed	peaceful	alarmed	daunted
silent	tranquil	anxious	scared
still	noiseless	nervous	terrified
calm	speechless	timid	intimidated
placid	taciturn	cowardly	fainthearted
soundless	mute	craven	chickenhearted

As they read they can note words that interest them, that make them *feel* the mood the writer wants them to feel. With experience they will see different ways in which writers express similar ideas. They may want to add phrases, sentences, even paragraphs to their collections.

When asked to describe a drab, tiresome, discouraging time we might use words such as *long, dull, boring, depressing.* C. S. Lewis said it was always winter but never Christmas. Enid Bagnold wrote, "On and on and on rolled the days, and though one might add them together and make them seven, they never made Sunday."

Figures of Speech

In the writer's kit bag there are special tools called figures of speech. These words and phrases are more than frivolous decorations used in literary discourse. They not only add color and imagery to speech and writing, but they are also a kind of shorthand, implying more than the words actually say, changing abstract ideas to pictures or experiences we all can relate to. They range from slang to the poetical and are as common in everyday speech as in fine writing.

As children begin to explore imaginative language they can learn the names for some of the figures of speech. The most commonly used figures are *simile, metaphor,* and *personification* (although *metaphor* is often used to mean any figurative language.)

"Metaphor," Theodore Bernstein wrote, "is just about as close as the average writer gets to creating poetry ... a kind of instant poetry."[4]

The simile can easily be identified as a comparison showing that something is *similar* to another thing: "like _____" or "as _____ ."

> fleece as white as snow
>
> smart like a fox
>
> happy as a lark
>
> working like a dog

Another figure of speech is the *metaphor.* The metaphor compares by saying one thing *is* another. If we say, "That tiger is *as tame as* a pussy cat," we are using a simile. If we say, "That tiger *is* a pussy cat!" we are using a metaphor.

> the moon is a gold coin
>
> he is a prince of a fellow
>
> the library is a treasure chest

Similes and metaphors are so common in our speech that we think of many of them—as in the examples above—as clichés, so it is important that we teach children to watch for bright, new comparisons, both in what they read and in what they hear.

Similes

"Magnificent Meanings"

(colors of importance to the Arapaho Indians)

White, Red, Black
White like a blizzard of snow
from the north.
Red like a youth
watching the east sun rise.
Black like old age
meeting the darkening western sky.

Naomi Hull
Sixth Grade

The wind tapped like a tired man.

Emily Dickinson

And tree and house, and hill and lake,
Are frosted like a wedding cake.

Robert Louis Stevenson

Metaphors

"Clouds"

White sheep, white sheep,
On a blue hill
When the wind stops
You all stand still.

Christina Rosetti

Orange is the smell of a
bonfire burning.
Pink is the beautiful
little sister of red.

Mary O'Neill

Books are ships which pass
through the vast seas
of time.

Francis Bacon

The third figure of speech children may come across in their reading is *personification*. Personification treats inanimate objects and abstract ideas as if they were animate, giving them life—often human—characteristics. Although personification is not found as often in today's stories and poems as in those of earlier times, this device can be useful if it is not overworked.

Personification

The drum's a very quiet fellow
When he's left alone.

John Farrar

Late lies the wintry sun a-bed,
A frosty, fiery sleepy-head.

Robert Louis Stevenson

The brook laughs louder when I come.

The leaves unhooked themselves from trees.

Emily Dickinson

The trees reached out with goblin arms
As black clouds frowned and grumbled.

KCP

Problems will arise when children experiment with figures of speech. First, children often misunderstand them or interpret them literally. Young children seem to be particularly talented in creating their own metaphors. Older children are often less spontaneous in their use of picturesque expressions, although Mary's simile came from the heart. At ten she was feeling a bit out of place with her teenage brothers and sister. "I feel," she said, "like a saucer with three dinner plates."

Three-year-old Johnny was sitting quietly with his eyes closed. When questioned, he answered, "I'm a burned-out light bulb." He didn't fare so well when he tried to use another term he'd heard. Finding a four-leaf clover, he announced, "See! I have pointed eyes!"

Children are frequently puzzled by expressions adults take for granted: a heart of stone, a stuffed shirt, a black sheep, a dark horse. When we ask children to observe and use figurative speech, we want to make sure they understand what the terms mean.

Other problems include putting in too much descriptive language, mixing images, and slipping into clichés. Lavish embellishments will not dress up a story or poem, but will, rather, distract from what the writer is trying to say. We can have too many comparisons, we can carry them too far for effectiveness, and, at times we can even mix them up. If we call a dangerous woman a tigress, then we must be careful not to go on and speak of victims rising to her bait or being caught in her web. If we have called the moon a gold coin let's not have the North Wind nibbling on it in the same sentence.

We have already mentioned similes that become clichés. Time-worn phrases will add nothing of interest to either writing or speech and will make both of them tiresome to the reader and listener. So, again, encourage students to look for new, unusual imagery in what they read, and then to try out imaginative comparisons in what they write.

Quiet as a Mouse?

Softly
Like snow falling on snow.

Anne Morrow Lindbergh

We shall walk in velvet shoes.

Elinor Wylie

Still as the hour-glass.

Dante Gabriel Rosetti

Thunders of white silence.

Elizabeth Barrett Browning

In a wonderful golden silence,
one of those musical silences
rich with the chiming of
unheard bells and the ring of
silent laughter.

Elizabeth Goudge

Older children might be interested in finding out more about figures of speech. Remembering their Greek-derived names is not important. Learning to use these devices can be entertaining now, of immeasurable help later. Here are nine other classifications:

allusion: indirect reference to something applicable to the subject — effective only when reader and writer share similar backgrounds (the troubles of a Job, the trials of a Tantalus)

analogy: basing comparison on similarities without actual or complete resemblance (Words are like pegs, to hang, not coats, but ideas on.)

euphemism: an inoffensive term used to avoid an unpleasant one (golden years, meaning old age; disadvantaged or underprivileged, meaning poor)

hyperbole: exaggeration (The Elephant's Child *"filled all Africa with his 'satiable curtiosities"* and sang down his trunk *"louder than several brass bands."*)

irony: using words to express the opposite of their literal meaning for humor or ridicule (The perfect birthday gift for Father: a billfold. A dillar, a dollar/A ten o'clock scholar,/What makes you come so soon?)

meiosos: understatement ("It'll do," meaning "Very good.")

litotes: a form of meiosos, an understatement in which an affirmative is expressed by a negative ("Not too bad," meaning "Very good.")

metonymy: using a name, attribute, or characteristic to mean the whole (the crown, meaning the ruler; colors, meaning the flag; Washington, meaning government)

synecdoche: a part standing for the whole (all hands on deck; a thousand head of cattle; the brains of the business) Sometimes the term *metonymy* will include *synecdoche.*

Slang

> What is called "slang" ... might well be regarded as the poetry of everyday life, since it performs much the same function as poetry; that is, it vividly expresses people's feelings about life and about the things they encounter in life.[5]
>
> S. I. Hayakawa

Slang words can be vigorous, colorful, and expressive. They can also be empty or *nothing* words. Some slang expresses so exactly what we mean that it becomes an accepted part of our language. (*Hoax* was slang in George Washington's day. *Strenuous* was considered a vulgar word in 1600, and it didn't become respectable until the twentieth century.) Other slang words are forgotten in a few years or even months. The meaning may change or vary in different localities. Judicious use of slang can add flavor and zip to writing. Overuse will only detract. Too much use of slang also restricts vocabulary growth by limiting the need for other words. The person addicted to the word *neat* may never learn to use such adjectives as *funny, exciting, attractive, interesting, mysterious, clever* — or even *tidy.*

THE SOUND OF WORDS

We have spoken before of the pleasure children find in the sounds of words. Now we want to look at ways we can use those sounds. When we talk of alliteration, onomatopoeia, rhyme, rhythm, and repetition we usually think of poetry, but these devices are important in prose writing, too.

Alliteration: the repetition of sounds at the beginning of words or in accented syllables

Diddle, diddle, dumpling

Wee Willie Winkie

tit for tat

spick and span

rough and ready

> *Sing a song of seasons!*
> *Something bright in all!*
> *Flowers in the summer,*
> *Fires in the fall!*
>
> Robert Louis Stevenson

Alliteration is as popular as an advertising technique as it is in children's story and verse. It is more commonly used in poetry, but it can be used—carefully—for emphasis in prose.

> *During the whole of a dull, dark, and*
> *soundless day in the autumn of the year ...*
>
> Edgar Allan Poe

> *In the days of the great Prince Arthur,*
> *there lived a mighty magician, called Merlin.*
>
> The History of Tom Thumb

Onomatopoeia: words that sound like their meaning:

bang	hum	clipclop
boom	hiss	howl
screech	fizz	murmur
clang	buzz	whine
tinkle	sizzle	twitter
varoom	crack	chirp
pop	slosh	cuckoo
ratatattat	crunch	whippoorwill

> tick tock
> sings the clock

> *The Rock-a-By Lady from Hush-a-By street*
> *Comes stealing; comes creeping....*
>
> Eugene Field

Rats!
They fought the dogs and killed the cats
...
And even spoiled the women's chats
By drowning their speaking
With shrieking and squeaking
In fifty different sharps and flats.
...
And the muttering grew to a grumbling;
And the grumbling grew to a mighty rumbling.

Robert Browning

I became aware of a distinct, hollow metallic,
and clangorous, yet apparently muffled reverberation.

Edgar Allan Poe

Rhyme: ending lines or words with an echoing sound. The repetition may be of the last syllables only, or of several syllables

Rhymes may be simple and uninvolved:

"Balloons"

Quietly drifting
In the air
People look
People stare
I have two
So I will share

Sabrina Singer
Sixth Grade

Or they may be as surprising as Lord Byron's:

Oh! ye lords of ladies intellectual,
Inform us truly, have they not henpecked you all?

Folktales and legends often have verses within the story. Children, in addition to writing poems, might like to use rhymes, or rhyming words or names, in the stories they write.

Fee, fi, fo fum!
I smell the blood of an Englishman!

Mirror, mirror on the wall,
Who is fairest of them all?

> *I'll huff and I'll puff*
> *And I'll blow your house in!*

> *"Where are you going, Henny-Penny,*
> *Cocky-Locky, Ducky-Daddles, and*
> *Goosey-Poosey?" says Turkey-Lurkey.*

For more on rhyming see chapter 10.

Rhythm and Repetition: "Rhythm ... is easy to understand, and not easy to define. In prose and poetry, it means the flow of accented and unaccented syllables," writes Clement Wood.[6]

We not only like the repetition of sounds, as in alliteration and rhyme, but a quick review of book, song, and play titles, slogans and expressions, indicates that we like the repetition of words and phrases, too.

Promises, Promises	bye-bye
One is One	so-so
Catch as Catch Can	fifty-fifty
Meet Me in Saint Louis, Louis	oh-oh

Repetition creates rhythm and rhythm is appealing — to the very young with their fondness for Pat-a-cake, Pat-a-cake, and to the more mature in their appreciation of rhetoric.

> *We cannot dedicate — we cannot consecrate —*
> *we cannot hallow — this ground.*

> Abraham Lincoln

> *Tomorrow, and tomorrow, and tomorrow,*
> *Creeps in this petty pace from day to day.*

> William Shakespeare

> *A time to weep, and a time to laugh;*
> *A time to mourn and a time to dance.*

> Ecclesiastes 3:4,
> King James Version

Rhythm does not depend on repetition, however, nor is it limited to poetry. "Four score and seven years ago" has a rhythm that makes the words easy to read and easy to remember. Opening lines of many stories, books, and plays are memorable because of their unobtrusive flow and cadence — their rhythm.

In a little village in New England there
was a little house which belonged to Mr. and Mrs.
Whittaker.

Robert Bright,
Georgie

"Christmas won't be Christmas without any presents."

Louisa May Alcott,
Little Women

It was dusk — winter dusk. Snow lay white and shining
over the pleated hills, and icicles hung from the forest
trees.

Joan Aiken,
The Wolves of Willoughby Chase

It was the best of times, it was the worst of times.

Charles Dickens,
A Tale of Two Cities

Now is the winter of our discontent
Made glorious summer by this sun of York.

William Shakespeare,
Richard III

By the sounds of the words we choose we can imply ideas without going into long descriptions. We can move our sentences as fast or as slowly as the action we're telling about. We can paint word pictures and create moods.

In "The Pied Piper of Hamelin" Robert Browning not only described the size and color of the rats, he showed us how they moved:

Grave old plodders, gay young friskers.

Grave, old, and *plodders* are not words one can hurry over. They give a weary, elderly feeling. *Gay, young*, and *friskers* not only imply youth, they are quick, lively words. Children can add *mood* words, *picture* words, to their lists.

hurry-up, action words		**slow and quiet words**	
hop	jump	hush	lazily
fly	leap	lullaby	silently
quick	slap	loiter	smoothly

Some letter sounds seem to imply certain moods:

joke	quiver	sleazy
jest	quaver	slimy
jolly	quake	slippery
joy	quail	slush
jovial		sludge
	query	
	question	
	quiz	

Perhaps Alexander Pope said it best in his *Essay on Criticism*.

'Tis not enough no harshness gives offense,
The sound must seem an echo to the sense:
Soft is the strain when Zephyr gently blows,
And the smooth stream in smoother numbers flows;
But when loud surges lash the sounding shore,
The hoarse, rough verse should like the torrent roar.

. . .

(Italics ours)

FUN WITH WORDS

Tom Sawyer said that work is what a body is *obliged* to do and play whatever a body is *not* obliged to do. The following activities could be considered play rather than work, games instead of exercises.

ABC and Rhyming Games

Probably the first word games we think of are ABC and rhyming games. Our grandparents played "Our Old Cat" and "When I Went Traveling—" and the versions and categories for this basic game are endless.

Our old cat is angry.
Our old cat is brave.

When I went traveling I took an apple.
When I went traveling I took a book.

Older children can add adjectives:

Our old cat is a clever creature.
When I went traveling I took a crumbly cracker.

Rhyming games can be as simple as lists or rhyming matches, or they can be more involved, such as the always popular Hinky-Pinky (or Stinky-Pinky) game. In this game a riddle is asked or a definition is given for which the answer will be two rhyming words with the same number of syllables. A hint is allowed, indicating the number of syllables in the answering words, by saying "Hink-Pink" or "Hinky-Pinky" or "Hinkety-Pinkety."

> What do you call a pan of boiling water? Hink-Pink.
> A hot pot.
>
> What do you call an attractive cat? Hinky-Pinky.
> Pretty kitty.
>
> What do voters give the losing candidate? Hinkety-Pinkety.
> An election rejection.
>
> What do you call an agricultural book-lender? Hink-hinkety-Pink-pinkety.
> An agrarian librarian.

Daffy Definitions

Making up amusing or silly definitions for unusual words can be fun, and it can also be motivation for using the dictionary in order to find the real meanings.

> *snickersnee: a type of clothing. I wore my new snickersnee to school today. — Chris*
>
> *orts: a green leafy vegetable. I just hate creamed orts but my mother serves them once a week. — Beth*
>
> *tonsorial: a sore throat caused by inflamed tonsils. I stayed home because I had a tonsorial infection. — Casey*
>
> *gossamer: a house for goslings. The farmer built a gossamer for the baby geese. — Kathie*

Dictionary Definitions

snickersnee: a knife, particularly one used as a weapon

orts: fragments of left-over food

tonsorial: pertaining to a barber or his work

gossamer: a gauzelike fabric (The origin of this word might be surprising.)

Made-up Words

> *"You see it's like a portmanteau — there are two meanings packed up into one word."*
>
> Lewis Carroll

Humpty Dumpty was explaining the meaning of words to Alice. Slithy, he said, was a combination of *lithe* and *slimy*. (And he also told her, "When I make a word do a lot of work like that, I always pay it extra.") "Centaur words," Theodore Bernstein called words like slithy, because, like the mythical animal, they usually combine the front end of one creature with the rear end of another.

Following are lists of words that do a lot of work—blend words and acronyms:

> brunch—breakfast and lunch
> motel—motor hotel
> smog—smoke and fog
> splutter—splash and sputter
> transistor—transfer and resistor

and another attributed to Lewis Carroll:

> chortle—chuckle and snort

Similar to blend words are *acronyms*—words made from the initials or syllables of a phrase. *Acronym* comes from two Greek words, *akros* meaning "tip" and *onyma* meaning "name." The experts don't agree on how large a tip may be used in making an acronym, so blend words are sometimes included. Acronyms are usually pronounced but some are spelled out. Many have been in our language for so long that we don't recognize them as such.

> AWOL—absent without leave
> COD—cash on delivery
> JEEP—GP, general purpose vehicle
> OK—some say from the misspelling, "Oll Korrect"
> RADAR—Radio Detection and Ranging
> SCUBA—self-contained underwater breathing apparatus
> UFO—unidentified flying object
> UNICEF—United Nations Children's Fund
> VIP—very important person
> ZIP—Zone Improvement Plan

The *Acronyms, Initialisms & Abbreviations Dictionary*[7] lists hundreds of these words, some well known, most quite unfamiliar. One of the longest words in the book is the acronym for Administrative Command, Amphibious Forces, Pacific Fleet, Subordinate Command: ADCOMSUBORDCOMPHIBSPAC.

SPELLING AND PRONUNCIATION

More word lists could include types of words such as homonyms and heteronyms. Some authorities are more specific in their classification of spell-alike and sound-alike words:

homographs — words spelled alike but pronounced differently
tear (as in ripping)
tear (as in weeping)

homonyms — words that are spelled alike but, because of difference in origins, have different meanings
bear (animal)
bear (to carry)

homophones — words that are not spelled alike but are pronounced the same way
peace and *piece*

We shall use the broader definition of homonym which includes homophone and the term heteronym instead of homograph.

Homonyms

words spelled differently but pronounced the same

air		heir
ceiling		sealing
cellar		seller
doe		dough
for	four	fore
great		grate
hole		whole
hour		our
kernel		colonel
made		maid
pray		prey
ring		wring
seam		seem
seen		scene
sight	site	cite
slay		sleigh
some		sum
wear		ware
write		right
wrote		rote

Heteronyms

words spelled the same but pronounced differently

close	close the door
close	stay close by
content	look for the content of the article
content	content and happy
entrance	the front entrance
entrance	the story will entrance you
lead	lead the way
lead	a lead pencil
minute	a minute amount
minute	wait a minute
read	I read now
read	I have read
refuse	I refuse to go
refuse	put the refuse in the trash can
row	raise a row and a rumpus
row	a row of corn; row a boat
wind	the wind blew
wind	wind the clock

Different pronunciations of the same letters and letter combinations are confusing, but they can be fun, too.

tough	heard	meat	rose	choke
bough	beard	great	lose	choir
cough	dread	threat		
slough				
mint	cork	card	do	pose
pint	work	ward	go	dose

With these words as suggestions students may even want to try some new spellings of old words themselves, as in the well-known spelling for fish, attributed to George Bernard Shaw:

gh as in tough = f
o as in women = i
ti as in motion = sh
so
ghoti = fish

x as in xylophone   = z
ough as in through = oo
so
xough = zoo

ch as in chorus   = c
eau as in beau   = o
kh as in khaki   = c
owe as in owe   = o
mn as in mnemonic   = n
ou as in tough   = u
th as in Thomas   = t
so
cheaukhowemnouth = coconut

When children play games and have fun with words they will develop a curiosity about words, become familiar with them, and, gradually, include them in their vocabulary. Understanding doesn't come with just looking words up in the dictionary. They must also be put to use.

PUTTING WORDS TO WORK

Ultimately writers are faced with the task
of selecting words and building them into
thought units that communicate with precision.

Dorothy Grant Hennings and
Barbara Grant[8]

Words by themselves can be interesting, curious, and fun. But writers must put together the best words in the best possible way if they are going to express their ideas effectively. Expanding sentences is a good exercise for learning how to put words to work.

The man walked up the street.

What kind of man? Young, old, happy, tired? What kind of street? A lane, a path, a city sidewalk? How did the man walk? Did he walk slowly—or did he stroll? Was he walking fast—or was he hurrying?

Nouns and verbs are the strongest words. Look first for nouns and verbs that can stand alone, that do not need to lean on adjectives or adverbs. In sixth grade Heather Aker wrote, "The cold of the early morning forced me to climb out of my warm bed *and shiver into my clothes.*"

Although they are necessary tools in our writer's kit bag, adverbs and adjectives are, at best, second best. Robert Gunning says, "Concrete, picturable verbs and nouns reflect facts and events as directly as it is possible for language to do so. Adjectives, on the other hand, always smell of opinion.... Readers and listeners always prefer fact to opinion."[9]

One thesaurus gives thirty-five terms that mean *moving slowly* and fifty-nine verbs—from *amble* to *wade*—that illustrate different ways of walking. It also gives nineteen adjectives synonymous with *old*, nine nouns ranging from *codger* to *patriarch* meaning *old man*, and fifty-nine synonyms for *road* or *street*.

It is not the most unusual or exotic or unexpected word that we look for. But if readers are to see as the writer sees, then it is important to find the exactly right word.

The strange man wore red clothes.

What kind of strange man do you see, and what kind of clothes?

I did not know this man wearing the maroon blazer.

or

The stranger wore cloak and pantaloons of scarlet.

Try also having students expand words and phrases into sentences:

> A pet—What kind of pet?
> A cat—What does it look like?
> A kitten—Long-haired. White.

> *The cat was on the mat.*
> *The kitten slept on the hearthrug.*
> *The fluffy white kitten dozed before the open fire.*

Add more details and expand the sentence into a paragraph.

A nice day.

What makes it a nice day? Is it sunny? Snowy? A birthday?

"It was a neat party. I had a good time."

All we know from those statements is that the speaker evidently enjoyed himself. *Neat, good, nice, pretty, beautiful, very, great* — these can be "nothing" words. They give, as Robert Gunning says, an opinion, but they conjure no pictures or sensory appeal. Discuss with children what makes a nice day? A neat party? A cozy room? An exciting book? A scary movie? With imaginations (and dictionary or thesaurus) filled with words, there is no need to settle for "The man walked up the street," "The strange man wore red clothes," — or, "It was a neat party."

As experiences grow, vocabularies grow, and then ideas grow. Ideas and thoughts develop one word at a time — words into sentences, sentences into paragraphs, paragraphs into stories. Without the proper word the idea is never expressed. In the beginning is the word.

Books to Read

Folsom, Franklin. *The Language Book.* New York: Grosset and Dunlap, Inc., Publishers, 1963.

Greet, W. Cabell, William A. Jenkins, and Andrew Schiller, eds. *In Other Words. A Junior Thesaurus.* Glenview, Ill.: Scott, Foresman and Company, 1969.

Nurnberg, Maxwell. *Wonders in Words.* Englewood Cliffs, N.J.: Prentice-Hall, Inc., 1968.

For teachers and older children:

Espy, Willard R. *An Almanac of Words at Play.* New York: Clarkson N. Potter, Inc., Publisher, 1975.

Holt, Alfred H. *Phrases and Word Origins.* New York: Dover Publications, Inc., 1961.

Sperling, Susan Kelz. *Poplollies and Bellibones.* New York: Clarkson N. Potter, Inc., Publisher, 1977.

NOTES

1. Frank Lloyd Wright, *A Testament* (New York: Horizon Press, 1957), 17.

2. Dorothy Grant Hennings and Barbara M. Grant, *Content and Craft — Written Expression in the Elementary School* (Englewood Cliffs, N.J.: Prentice-Hall, Inc., 1973), 123. Used with permission of Dorothy Grant Hennings.

3. Mauree Applegate, *Freeing Children to Write* (New York: Harper & Row, 1963), 10.

4. Theodore M. Bernstein, *The Careful Writer* (New York: Atheneum Publishers, 1973), 275.

5.   S. I. Hayakawa, *Language in Thought and Action*, 4th ed. (Orlando, Fla.: Harcourt Brace Jovanovich, Inc., 1978), 111.

6.   Clement Wood, ed., *The Complete Rhyming Dictionary and Poet's Craft Book* (Garden City, N.J.: Garden City Publishing Company, Inc., 1936), 7.

7.   Ellen T. Crowley and Helen E. Sheppard, eds., *Acronyms, Initialisms & Abbreviations Dictionary*, 9th ed. (Detroit: Gale Research Company, 1984).

8.   Dorothy Grant Hennings and Barbara Grant, *Written Expression in the Language Arts*, 2nd ed. (New York: Teachers College Press, 1982), 189. Used with permission of Dorothy Grant Hennings.

9.   Robert Gunning, *The Technique of Clear Writing* (New York: McGraw-Hill Book Company, Inc. Copyright, 1952 by Robert Gunning), 102.

eight

Research and Nonfiction Writing

*Facts are to the mind
what food is to the body.*

For all knowledge and wonder (which is the seed of knowledge) is an impression of pleasure in itself.

Francis Bacon

Facts are to the mind what food is to the body.

Edmund Burke

As teachers, one of the most rewarding ideas to which we can expose children is the joy of learning new things. Add to this joy of learning the joy of finding it out for yourself — the element of discovery through research — and we have developed lifelong students. From there we go to the desire to share new learning with others, and reports, magazine and newspaper articles become exciting communication devices.

All children find the idea of being a detective exciting. Let them become involved in detecting interesting facts, anecdotes about people and history, whims and oddities of nature. Too often children are impatient and copy lengthy notes from the first things they read — probably encyclopedias. Give plenty of time for browsing and poking through materials, immersing themselves in books and old magazines, musing over facts and figures, pictures, ads, maps, and mysteries of the past and future. Praise planning and thinking — then the original research which involves gathering a number of sources and making deductions about the material.

RESEARCH: To look again.

Have children re-search material for new ideas. Look again. And not just at books and magazines, but pictures, films, actual sites. Interview or write letters to experts. Write for government publications, a wealth of free and inexpensive offerings prepared by experts and in the public domain. Children tend to think research involves burying oneself in a dusty library for weeks. Talk about types of research, creative research projects they can find out about.

Nonfiction is as exciting and often stranger than fiction. Some real happenings would not be believable in a story. Many things that were once fiction are now fact. Jules Verne wrote of going to the moon and living under the ocean. We can now read of the actual adventures of explorers making these trips.

Creative Assignment

Compare how men went to the moon in the book *From the Earth to the Moon* by Jules Verne and how men actually went to the moon. What things were different? The same? Can you find any facts that were available at the time Verne wrote the story that helped him speculate on men going to the moon? Think of technology available to people today. What adventures do you think will become fact fifty years from now? One hundred years?

Read *Twenty Thousand Leagues under the Sea* by Jules Verne and compare it to the exploration men are doing under the ocean today.

Read Arthur C. Clarke's *Dolphin Island* and *Man and Dolphin* by John C. Lilly. How did Clarke use the real research that is going on with dolphins to write a fiction story? What facts did he use? A writer can take facts and stretch (extrapolate) them to make a fiction story ring true.

For older students: Read *The Day of the Dolphin* by Robert Merle and see how he used dolphin research to create an exciting fiction story. Lead a class discussion on this technique, thinking of other fiction books that are based on facts. Write a story stretching fact into the future so that it will seem possible for your story to someday come true. At the end of the story tell what facts you used and why you think your story might be possible.

Creative Assignment

Have research contests using the following suggestions or others:

Most interesting or obscure fact about Abraham Lincoln, Teddy Roosevelt, etc.

World Record Book of Animal Facts

Funny inventions of the past

Most unusual fish/bird/animal

Most unusual fish/bird/animal behavior

Most unusual plant fact/behavior

Best true ghost story

Most interesting supernatural event

All research must be documented to win.

REPORTS

The nonfiction written in most classrooms comes in the form of reports. And how often are these reports shared only with a teacher? We are not advocating doing away with reports, but making them more creative. Children seem to respond best to a writing task when it has a meaning. Writing a report only for an assignment or a grade isn't enough. Reports should be widely shared, enjoyed for good writing technique as well as quality research.

Guide to Writing Creative Reports

Choose a topic.

Question yourself about the topic.

Brainstorm all that you know or all you'd like to know about the topic.

Research for facts.

Choose which facts to use.

Choose which facts to leave out.

Organize the material.

Write so the reader says, "I didn't know that!"

CLASSROOM MAGAZINES

In addition to reports introduce a class magazine as an integral part of a classroom's curriculum. Magazine writing can develop and hone a child's writing skills as well as motivate him to provide a quality publication for his classmates. He knows he is writing something to share with others.

We have several suggestions for the magazine make-up:

1. The magazine could remain the same throughout the year, copying the style of a general interest publication. The Fourth Grade Review. The Friday Evening Post. In this case contents could consist of: articles of general interest, personality articles on interesting students, teachers, and parents; how-to articles, poetry, fiction, puzzles, games and quizzes. Change editors occasionally—monthly—with all students contributing.

2. The magazine could change design monthly or every six weeks, following curriculum units. After a nature unit the class could publish a Ranger Rick type of nature magazine. To culminate a unit on airplanes, the publication is Aviation Views covering articles on history and future of flying, profiles of famous flyers and planes and airports, stories and poetry about travel and flying. Games, quizzes, puzzles can follow the same subject matter.

3. Perhaps by second semester the class could divide up into three groups, each publishing a different magazine.

In any case, with this format the children are always writing for a peer audience and can take pride in editing and polishing in order to communicate well. Be sure all children are contributing and sharing the responsibility and work. Contributions of fiction and poetry should be on a volunteer basis. So many children are interested in the idea of having their material published— perhaps a parent-motivated idea. A classroom magazine will satisfy this need.

THE DIFFERENT TYPES OF ARTICLES AND HOW TO WRITE THEM

The How-to Article

1. Choose a project that is fresh and new and of interest to the reader. Why would the reader want to make or to do this? 2. State what materials are needed. Give suggestions for free or inexpensive materials that will work. 3. List or explain what could go wrong—the pitfalls. 4. Give process or procedure. 5. Tell the happy result.

What ideas can children have for how-tos? There are children expert in many areas. Here are a few suggestions:

> How to Make Extra Spending Money
>
> How to Raise Gerbils, Tropical Fish, etc.
>
> Stamp Collecting Is Fun
>
> How to Use Stamps to Illustrate Your Reports
>
> How to Make a Paper Airplane That Will Really Fly
>
> Kites with Original Designs
>
> How to Make and Keep Friends
>
> How to Get Along with Your Mother/Father/Sister/Brother
>
> Pet Care Made Easy
>
> So You Have a New Puppy (Kitten)
>
> Do You Really Want Your Own Horse?
>
> Math Made Easy
>
> Bicycle Safety
>
> Raise House Plants for Fun and Inexpensive Gifts
>
> A Gift You Can Make without Spending Much Money
>
> Making Use of the School Library
>
> How to Make School More Fun.

The Personality Article

Many students, parents, and teachers have interesting hobbies, talents, and skills, or achievements that will fascinate the whole class.

How to Interview: Make an appointment with the subject. Find out what you can ahead of time so you will have something to talk about. List questions you want to ask. If you are interviewing someone who raises tropical fish, for example, ask to see his collection. You will find out a lot by observing. If you are interviewing a teacher who writes books, read some of her books before you talk to her. Use a tape recorder or write down interview notes as soon as you have finished talking. Try not to write notes the whole time you are talking with a person. Listen and remember. (Practice on a classmate.) Be sure to thank the person you interview and send him a copy of the article you write.

The History Article

Seek out unknown facts or interesting happenings. Write so the reader says, "I didn't know that!" Use fiction technique to dramatize a moment in history. Why is this interesting today? Is anything similar happening today? For instance, are there similarities in going West to settle new territory and going under the ocean to live? Have you ever thought when you serve ice cream at your birthday party that Dolley Madison first made it popular by serving it at a party at the White House? Try to show your classmates why history means something in their lives today.

Creative Assignment

Bring history to life with "You Are There" stories. You are there with George Washington during that terrible winter at Valley Forge. How do you feel? What do you see? What is happening? The Boston Tea Party. The Signing of the Declaration of Independence.

Writing Book Reviews

A book review is often more fun to read and to write than a book report. Have you ever spent an hour comparing book lists and favorite authors with a new friend? Sharing a book — reading and persuading others to read it — is a part of the joy of literature. Suggestions for writing a book review: 1. A short summary of the book. Don't tell the ending! 2. Why do you think the author wrote it, or where did he get his idea? 3. How it differs from other books on the same subject. 4. Why you did or didn't like the book. 5. Why the reader should or shouldn't read it. Perhaps someone in the class would like to write an on-going new-book column.

Quizzes

Children like a challenge. They also like to laugh. Humor helps to impress a fact on the memory. They like to think, figure out, and solve. Quizzes can be creative for both reader and writer and also a fun and painless way to learn any subject.

Washington threw the following object across the Rappahannock.
1. a stone   2. his shoes   3. the boat paddles

Paul Revere was
1. a veterinarian   2. a silversmith   3. a house painter

A standard unit of measurement is called a
1. slice   2. yard   3. length

Quizzes can also be designed to teach children to make decisions or think out solutions to problems, teaching them concepts.

Your best friend has started smoking in secret. You should
1. tell the teacher
2. try to talk him out of it
3. smoke with him so he won't think you're chicken
4. ask the teacher to have a unit on smoking so he can learn the hazards to his health

Number four is of course the right answer, but in telling the correct answer, the quiz should review why the other answers are not good, unless it is obvious.

Puzzles

A challenging way to use words for spelling and vocabulary enrichment is crossword puzzles, acrostics, and hidden word puzzles. Both the creator and the person who works the puzzle learn. Let children find other types of puzzles from magazines or books or design their own.

Dot to dot (to find an extinct animal, for instance)

Hidden objects (Five products of Brazil are hidden in this picture.)

Brain teasers

Original riddles

Mazes

Survey Articles

Pick a question that is controversial or involves what people think or feel or remember. Interview about a dozen people and you have an article. Some suggested subjects are:

What is our school's biggest problem?

What is your favorite subject in school and why?

If you were a teacher, what would you do differently?

If you were president of the United States what would you do?

If you could make an announcement to the children of the world, what would you tell them?

If you had a million dollars what would you do with it?

What is your favorite holiday and why?

What was your most remembered Christmas?

What was the worst trouble you were ever in?

Your most embarrassing moment?

Students may also write letters to do a survey. For instance, a student might write to authors asking why they like to write. Or movie stars about their most embarrassing moments. Be sure to have students write more letters than they think they need for an article. Not everyone will answer the letter.

The Personal Article

Many things that happen in everyday life are interesting to others when told in a creative, humorous way or in a way which helps someone else with the problem or experience related in the article. There should be a universal element in the article—one to which everyone could relate.

Some examples of personal articles that children can write are:

My Earliest Memory

Our Family Bike Trips

What I Like to Do Best after School

Things That Scare Me

Articles about favorite sports, hobbies, pets, etc.

The Person I Admire Most

The Hardest Thing I Ever Did

The Art of Being Alone (And Enjoying It)

Be Yourself

Adults with Whom I Feel Comfortable and Why

My Favorite Adult

Travel Articles

Children today travel a great deal. Instead of "What I Did on My Summer Vacation" writers can share places they have been. Use these tips for writing a travel article. 1. Where we went—not just the facts—let the reader see the place. 2. What was interesting there? 3. Why would someone else want to go there? 4. Pictures?

Photo Essay

The photo essay is very popular in today's magazines. Older children may use cameras and combine photographs with captions. Younger children may draw pictures and caption them for an article. Be sure the writers keep their pictures in the correct order to tell the facts. How-to articles may be done in this manner as well.

SOME GENERAL RULES FOR WRITING ARTICLES

1. Choose a subject someone else would want to read about. If the reader says, "So what!" when he finishes an article, the writer has misjudged the universality of his idea.

2. Don't make the article too broad or too general. Focus on a narrow subject. Choosing World War II as a subject for a five hundred word article will give the writer trouble from the beginning.

3. Write to a word limit. This makes you choose important words and cut a rambling style. Learning to write in a clean, crisp, sparse style is a skill that will serve in future school work.

4. Write in a clear and interesting manner. Don't show off how much you know about the subject.

5. Relate the article to the reader if possible. (The "you" approach.)

Make research fun and nonfiction come alive for your students. Challenge them to read and write, sharing knowledge. Look for originality of research and ideas as you would pan for gold.

nine

Letter Writing

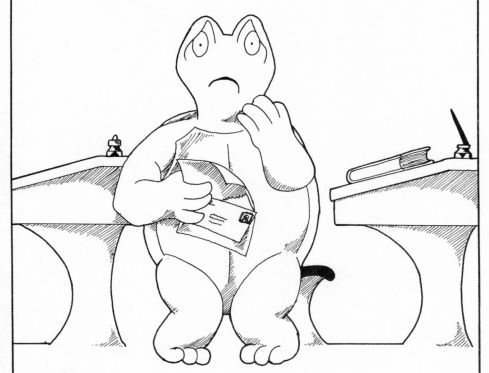

Dear Garth,
*   Do you want to fight tonight? if you*
do just give a little wisil....

> The writing we need most in life—the writing of letters and notes—is least stressed in school.... The alarming number of Americans who do all their communicating by mail with greeting cards ... should point out to the schools the necessity for the letter-writing habit.
>
> Mauree Applegate[1]

In this world of telephones and cassettes—and greeting cards—there is still a need for writing letters. We all, from time to time, should be able to communicate by written word, clearly and graciously. Often we can express our ideas best in writing because of the thought and reflection we give to what we want to say. And, conversely, an impromptu note, tucked into a pocket or scribbled on an assignment paper, can bring as much pleasure as a formal letter delivered by the postman.

This chapter presents ideas for making letter writing interesting and rewarding. There are suggestions for teaching children how to write business letters that are courteous, clear, and brief; examples showing how personal letters can express personal feelings; and, yes, some ideas and occasions for making and sending greeting cards.

Letter writing can be one of the most creative of the forms of creative writing because it becomes an ongoing project. A letter written implies an answer written. But how to get that first letter actually written and how to write it so it will inspire an answer—these are the objectives of classroom letter writing.

MOTIVATION AND INSPIRATION

Passing Notes

Receiving notes of appreciation from parents and teachers could possibly do more to encourage children's note and letter writing than any number of formal lessons on "the friendly letter," or post-Christmas or birthday threats. Receiving an unexpected note can be the high point of a day—whether it is delivered by the postman or "by hand," written on the margin of a math paper, or come upon in an out-of-the-way place. (Once, when dusting, one of us found inside a vase a slip of paper that said, "I LOVE YOU.")

As school children, we never understood why passing notes was considered such a heinous crime. Perhaps if parents and teachers would initiate note-passing it would become acceptable (and lead to the writing of longer letters).

For example:

A note slipped inside a notebook, a desk, or laid on a pillow—

Thank you for running that errand for me today. You really helped me out.

On a margin or clipped to an assignment or a piece of personal writing—

I appreciate the time and work you have put in on this report.

or

The class enjoyed this when you read it aloud, and I'm glad to have had time to re-read it. Thank you for making this subject so interesting to all of us.

or

Thank you for sharing this with me.

And, in return, we can hope that children will learn to say little thank-you's—

Here is the paper I owe you. Thanks for lending me some.

or

Thank you for finishing Charlotte's Web today instead of having spelling.

Thank-you Letters

Writing thank-you letters may always be more duty than delight, but developing the habit of writing little thank-you's will at least make the task easier. The three points to remember in teaching children to write thank-you letters are:

1. They—the writers—should say *thank you.*

2. They should express appreciation for the giver's thinking of them.

3. They should never be so truthful as to hurt the giver's feelings, but neither should they be forced to be insincere. ("It's *just* what I *always* wanted.")

Letters acknowledging gifts that are something less than hoped-for can be looked upon as real challenges for creative writing.

Greeting Cards

While we have already indicated a lack of enthusiasm for conducting *all* correspondence by means of mass-produced, commercial greeting cards, individually designed, personal greeting cards can be fun to make and to receive. For very young children these may *be* their letters. Older children can use greeting cards as ways of sharing artwork, poems, or brief prose pieces. The important point here is for children to understand that an artist and verse writer miles away cannot always express our own personal feelings better than we can. Sometimes commercial cards are exactly right. Sometimes they aren't.

MAKING LETTERS INTERESTING

While etiquette books are still telling us that letters should be written in blue or black ink on white stationery that is preferably undecorated, either by manufacturer or letter writer, the books do not tell us how to make letter writing fun. One answer to that might be to leave the etiquette-book rules for adults to follow or break. Colored pens, colored paper, illustrations—pictures drawn, or cut from newspapers or magazines and mounted on the writing paper—all can help to make what has traditionally been considered a task into a creative project.

Of course, letters, even if written on pink paper with red ink or orange paper with black ink, will still be dull if they are *how-are-you-I-am-fine* types. Just as they have learned to do in their other kinds of writing, children should make their letters interesting, colorful, and thoughtful. They should write neatly and proofread after writing.

Every year irate people write articles and columns, even letters to Ann Landers and Abby Van Buren, complaining about the long, boring Christmas letters they receive. Could it be that these letters make the recipients unhappy because too many of them are nonstop monologues of I, Me, Mine, We, Us, Ours? Letters can seem more like conversation if they include some recognition of the reader:

What do you think—

I remember that you said (did)—

That day you and I—

Think of a letter as a visit. Set the scene or mood:

It's cold and snowy today—the sort of day to stay indoors.
So I thought it would be a good time for a visit with you.

or

> *I had the most fantastic thing happen to me today, and I've*
> *just got to tell you about it right now!*

Letters don't necessarily have to be limited to facts and happenings. They can include some thoughts and ideas, interesting or amusing clippings, verse, recommendations and opinions about books, movies, television programs:

> *Remember the day we went to the zoo and saw the lion*
> *sleeping on his back with his paws in the air? When I saw*
> *this picture in the paper I just had to send it to you.*

or

> *I just finished reading <u>Meet the Austins</u> by Madeleine*
> *L'Engle. It made me think of when your Aunt died. I hope*
> *you'll read it.*

or

> *My father found this verse in a magazine. He said it*
> *reminded him of you.*

And remember, if letters are to be conversations and not monologues, questions should be answered and more questions should be asked:

> *Yes! Yes! Yes! It's absolutely my very, all-time, more than*
> *any, favorite program, too!*

or

> *I still don't know if I'm going to camp or not. There's a*
> *chance I might make the summer swim team. I'll let you*
> *know as soon as I can.*

or

> *Did you ever talk your mother into letting you take guitar?*
> *If you had to make a choice (like me) would you go out for*
> *soccer or take karate lessons?*

A creatively written letter will bring the writer to the reader. It will make the reader see as the writer sees and feel as the writer feels. Such letters will also make readers want to respond with what they think and see and feel. Creative letter writing brings individuals closer together by bringing their lives and their worlds closer together.

RECEIVING LETTERS

For children of any age who have never been sent mail, getting letters with their own names on them can make a subtle difference. They become people of importance, people who receive mail.

For many children, discovering the pleasure of receiving "real mail" may be the first step towards understanding the rewards of letter writing. As a beginning, a classroom post office can give them the practice of writing and the pleasure of receiving their own personal letters.

Creative Assignment

Let the children set up a post office within the classroom. After they have had experience in exchanging letters with their classmates, try expanding the project in various ways:

1. Appoint or elect postal clerks for limited time periods.

2. Have a one-time letter exchange, or

3. choose classroom pen pals for a week.

4. Exchange letters with another class.

5. Exchange letters with another school.

As with any exchange, the teacher must make sure every child is included and that the letter writing doesn't turn into some sort of popularity contest.

PEN PALS

Letters to pen pals need to be considered a little differently from informal notes to friends, classmates, and gift-giving adults. The pen-pal letter, especially if it is going abroad, speaks not just for the child who writes it, but also represents his school, town, state—even his country. For this reason these letters should be written with thoughtful planning, checked for correct grammar and spelling, and neatly recopied.

The writer introduces herself, tells something about her family, school, community, pets, hobbies. She asks questions that will show her interest in the pen pal and where he lives but that are not too personal. When a child decides to write to a pen pal parents and teachers should encourage her to keep the correspondence going.

BUSINESS LETTERS

A Business Call

Chambers of Commerce and companies that have promotional material available occasionally comment that some letters they receive from school children are sloppily written, unclear, or even rude, with never so much as a please or a thank you.

If personal letters are considered visits with friends, then the business letter could be looked upon as a business call to an office or place of work. Children's business letters do not need to be formal or stilted, but, just as with a face-to-face interview, there are certain points of etiquette to observe.

Talk Session

Teacher:	If you needed to get some information from a business person, how would you go about it?
Child:	I'd go to his office.
Child:	I'd telephone him.
Teacher:	All right. Now you are in his office, or you have reached him by telephone. Now what?
Child:	I'd tell him who I am—
Child:	—and what I wanted.
Child:	And why I needed to know.
Teacher:	Would you talk about the weather or how the Cubs or the Cardinals are doing?
Child:	No, of course not.
Teacher:	Why not?
Child:	Because the man is busy—
Child:	—and I don't want to take up his—or *her*—time.
Teacher:	After he has told you what you need to know what will you do?
Child:	Leave.
Child:	Say good-bye.
Child:	Thank the person for helping me.
Teacher:	If you are as polite and thoughtful as you've said you would be, what do you suppose the business person will think about you?
Child:	That I'm polite.
Child:	He'll be glad he could help me.
Child:	He'll feel good and I'll feel good.
Teacher:	Suppose you can't visit or reach this business person by telephone. Suppose he is hundreds of miles away. What would you do then?
Children:	Write a letter!
Teacher:	How, in a letter, can you make him feel good about helping you?
Child:	Be polite.
Child:	Be sure the letter is neat.
Child:	—words spelled right—
Child:	—explain what you want—
Child:	—and why you want it.
Child:	Say thank you.
Child:	And say please—

A letter saying, "Rush me all you kno on youaniym minening...." is not going to give a good impression of the child who sends it or of the school he represents. Nor will it inspire the receiver to cooperate in rushing anything.

Creative Assignment

Children, as individuals or as a class, can write to

government officials, town or state, with questions, suggestions, or thank-you letters for services or accomplishments manufacturers, about products they like or dislike

television and radio broadcasting companies, producers, program sponsors, about programs they like or dislike

companies that offer informational material free or for a minimum fee

A Soft Answer ...

... turns away wrath, but a harsh word stirs up anger.

Letters of complaint should be composed with special care. While anger and disappointment may be the strongest feelings of the writer, an angry accusation will most often provoke angry feelings, and then an angry, or at least an indifferent, answer. It is often difficult not to express one's true feelings. But a letter written thoughtfully, explaining the problem in straightforward, polite words, even with a touch of humor, will be the letter that receives the quickest, most satisfactory answer.

BOOKS THAT CAN MOTIVATE LETTER WRITING

Below are listed some books that give names, addresses, and information about companies that offer free material for young people of various ages and interests. For more information see your library's copy of *Books in Print*.

When the letter writer is asking for an answer, information, or a small pamphlet from any individual or company, it is courteous to enclose a stamped, self-addressed number ten envelope for the reply. Some answers may never arrive unless the self-addressed, stamped envelope (referred to as SASE) is included. If extra postage is required, the source will usually say so.

Feinman, Jeffrey, ed. *Freebies for Kids.* New York: Wanderer Books, 1979.

Grady, Tom, ed. *Free Stuff for Cooks.* Wayzata, Minn. 55391: Meadowbrook Press.

Hehner, Barbara, and Louise Delagran, eds. *Free Stuff for Kids.* Musson, 1983.

Lansky, B., and Tom Grady, eds. *Free Stuff for Kids,* revised ed. Wayzata, Minn. 55391: Meadowbrook Press, 1981.

Pepe, Thomas J., ed. *Free & Inexpensive Educational Aids,* 4th ed. New York: Dover Publications, Inc., 1970.

United States Government. Superintendent of Documents. *Consumer Information Catalog.* Consumer Information Center, Department K, Pueblo, Colo. 81009.

Weiss, Jeffrey. *Free Things for Campers and Other Lovers of the Outdoors.* New York: G. P. Putnam's Sons, 1982.

LETTERS THAT WILL NEVER BE SENT

Another experiment in letter writing can be composing letters that are never mailed. These letters are written to fictional characters, historical figures, or even inanimate objects:

> *Dear Georgie,*
> *You are my favorite ghost. I wish you lived at my house....*

or

> *Dear President Washington,*
> *There's a story going around that you chopped down your father's cherry tree and then said, "I cannot tell a lie." Is it true that....*

or

> *Dear Old-friend Bicycle,*
> *I hope you understand why I have to sell you and get a new, bigger bike. We've had some mighty good times together....*

A POSTSCRIPT

As with all their personal writing, children's right to privacy in their letter-writing should be meticulously protected. Unless an assignment is specifically for letters to be shared, that option should be the child's choice.

Although we hope that business and pen-pal letters will be neat and correct, as a rule, children's letters should not be rewritten and rewritten until they are examples of perfect spelling, grammar, and penmanship—unless, for some unusual reason, they are needed for examples of perfect spelling, grammar, and penmanship.

Most of the adults who receive children's letters will appreciate far more the charm of the first or, at most, the second draft with its spontaneity and misspellings. Children receiving letters from other children will be more interested in the content and the fact that they have received a real letter than they will be with grammatical and spelling perfection. Whatever they are writing, children should be allowed—no, *encouraged*—to develop their own styles and to speak in their own voices.

> *Dear Garth,*
>   *Do you want to fight tonight? if you do just give a little wisil and I'll be write on your tell but I don't think you will go home the way you came. if your mother ask you what happen tell her that a sikelone struck you. don't forget tonight.*
>   *Your hatful Friend,*
>   *Donald*
>
>   (Fourth grade)

NOTES

1. Mauree Applegate, *Freeing Children to Write* (New York: Harper & Row, 1963), 100.

ten

Catching Poems

From his pot of words a poet selects as few as possible and builds a poem.

"A Poem"

A poem is a rock
Getting thrown into an ocean,
Hitting a seashell in a wave,
Sinking further and further
    into the sand.
A poem stops
And gets dug back up
Only to get thrown in again.

A poem is a memory.
One that goes back in years.
A poem is laughing at
The fun of that memory.
A poem is making more
Memories.

Rick Wehner
Age eleven

Poetry is hard to define. Perhaps we should not try. It is a special type of creative writing. Maxwell Bodenheim says poetry is the impish attempt to paint the color of the wind. George Meredith calls it talking on tiptoe. Another definition is an emotion remembered in tranquility. It is hard to write about anything you are angry about, sad about, dreamy about, when the emotion still envelopes you. But when your mind is relaxed, thoughts fly in unbidden.

If children think of the word "catching" along with the word "poem," poetry doesn't seem so overwhelming, so esoteric. Poems can be caught when one is baking, driving a car, showering, waking up in the morning—the unlikeliest times.

Sometimes these "poems caught when you least expected them" rhyme, but more often they are free verse. Sometimes you catch a piece of a poem and have to add to it later.

"Rain"

When it rains
Your raincoat gets wet.
When you fall in puddles
<u>*You*</u> *get wet.*

Freddie
Age eight

Ashley
jumped up
and kissed me
good morning
on my nose.
But I wasn't even up.

Rebecca
Age nine

In writing poetry children should try to paint a picture with their words so that someone sees what they've seen, feels something they've felt. Freshness and creativity, originality, is the quality to aim for when catching poems. Children look at the world with such wonder and freshness that if they can be spontaneous, not work too hard at writing poetry, their poems will delight the reader.

Who else but a child would think that violets smell purple or that sadness is a remote isle where happy never touches or laziness is the art of doing nothing? It is adults who more often write clichés.

Writing poetry is a good time for children to learn to play with words. Squeeze them up. Stretch them out. Look for sound words because poetry is written to be read aloud. Discover the music of words and poetry.

Creative Assignment

Have children make posters for the poetry-writing corner. Use these captions:

A poet looks at things in a different manner.

A poet looks inside the world.

A poet looks inside herself for how she feels about the world.

A poet thinks about feelings.

From his pot of words a poet selects as few as possible and builds a poem.

A poem touches feelings deep inside another person.

Get inside your world—share it with a poem.

FREE VERSE

Robert Frost has said that writing free verse is like playing tennis without a net. This poetry is written with a flexible form, no regular rhyme, meter, or stanzas, but poets have to discipline their words or they will have chaos. Some children find writing good free verse more difficult than verse with form, but in free verse emotion becomes uppermost. Choice of words is stressed. The child has to say his thought in as few words as possible so that each word is important. Line breaks help us to read the poem, but the poet must think about where to break the line, since the last word in the sentence stands out, and is usually most important. Sometimes a line consists of one word. Putting that one word on a line draws attention to it, so it must be important and also the right word.

Why write free verse instead of prose? Saying something in a poetic manner often moves us, makes us experience stronger feelings than prose could do. Read the poetry below — free verse. Dea could have said in an essay that some children in other parts of the world are starving. She could say families are breaking apart because of the refugee situation. We would have heard it; we might have cared; but note the strength of emotion evoked by saying it her way. Notice how she arranged the words to stress importance. (These poems were written after Dea looked at pictures of refugee families.)

> *The child looked into the distance,*
> *bright, brown eyes dulling*
> *her round stomach was huge.*
> *She was suffering.*
> *I can see the pain in her face.*
> *She cries out in anguish.*
> *She hasn't seen food in weeks*
> *her life is dwindling*
> *slowly, fading*
> *gone.*

Dea Hynes
Age fourteen

> *we look into each other's eyes*
> *we little ones hold each other's hands*
> *we learn together*
> *we cry together*
> *we share joy,*
> *sorrow,*
> *hunger,*
> *we live*
> *we die*
> *we love one another*
> *life.*

Dea Hynes

when will I see you again?
my baby sister is gone
when did she go?
the trees enfold us
through our journey
through life
through malnutrition
through death

Dea Hynes

Activity

After a brainstorming or talk session, have children write an essay on some subject. Select a couple of essays and read them. Then on the board, show the class how the essay could be rewritten as free verse by selecting the most important words to say the same thing.

After a talk session on endangered species: *"I think that we should leave them in their natural habitat. I also think that we (as in all the people) should stop hunting animals so we don't kill all the animals because if we do we (humans) will die also."*

Chris
Age ten

Leave them.
Leave them there
in their natural habitat.
We, all the people,
We
should
stop
stop hunting.
If we kill
all
all the animals,
We, all the people,
We
will also die.

Karin's prose is so poetic it can be arranged almost as it is for free verse:

"When I was young I thought the moon was a reflection of the earth and that it was really flat and thin like tissue paper."

Karin Krauth
Age eleven

When I was young
I thought
The moon was a reflection
of earth.
Flat,
Thin,
Like tissue paper.

POETRY WITH FORM

We have not attempted to teach children such sophisticated forms of poetry as sonnets and ballads, although some children would probably enjoy the challenge. But children should learn form and meter. There are easier forms to start with and have fun with. Here are a few which we have found successful. Teachers should always be on the lookout for other types.

Haiku

This Japanese poetry is very popular with both teachers and children. Seventeen syllables long, the lines are traditionally written as in these examples.

The sun, barely seen
Rising over morning dawn
Dew drops melt quickly.

Dea Hynes
Age fourteen

On a summer day
I listen to the ocean
I smell the salt breeze.

Ben
Age eleven

The lines may be any length, however, and occasionally come out to sixteen or eighteen syllables.

The baby frog swam
in my friend's aquarium
not even an inch long.

Hellen Munro
Age eight

Haiku is classified as image poetry, the verse bringing to the reader's mind a picture or a feeling. Images come from three places:

1. The senses: here and now vision and experience.

2. The memory: stored in the mind.

3. The fantasy: invented in the mind.

In introducing Japanese poetry bring to class brush paintings by Japanese artists. With as few strokes as possible the artist creates a picture. With as few words as possible one can also paint a word picture. Think of a camera taking a picture. An image is frozen in time. Haiku is traditionally nature poetry, but children use the form for other images.

> *A cat comes into*
> *my garden, ignoring me.*
> *She knows the world is hers.*
>
> Kirsten Wayland
> Age thirteen

> *A goldfish gapes in surprise.*
> *He has just encountered*
> *the stone man in his pool.*
>
> Kirsten Wayland

> *in the morning*
> *A flower blooms*
> *born is a glory*
> *to the world.*
>
> Caitlin McDonnell
> Age eleven

> *Fright*
> *The door creaks open.*
> *Slowly, slow, something creeps out.*
> *I wake. What a dream!*
>
> Heather Aker
> Age ten

Tanka

Tanka, like the haiku, is over five hundred years old. Like the haiku, tanka makes use of the five-seven syllable approach except that the verse itself is thirty-one syllables long. Sometimes the first and second lines are related, as well as the third and fourth, and the fifth line is a refrain or a line that pulls the two ideas together (five-seven; five-seven; seven). But other groupings of the syllables are also possible.

> *Water flows down softly,*
> *Glides through a cool waterfall.*
> *Refreshing wetness.*
> *Like a little butterfly,*
> *Floating slowly in the wind.*
>
> Melissa
> Age eleven

Abandoned, the park
is quiet, very silent.
  things get very dim.
Old leaves scuttle in the wind
After the people have gone.

Jackie Olsen
Age thirteen

STANZA PATTERNS OF RHYMED VERSE

A group of lines arranged formally as a part of a poem is called a stanza. Stanzas may be any number of lines and are named accordingly.

Couplet

The couplet is a two-line stanza. The two lines rhyme. The lines should be about the same length.

Classy
Lassy

Ghosts are the very most.
I don't want to be their host.

Jerry
Age nine

Tercet

A tercet is a three-line stanza. Usually all three lines follow the same rhyme sound.

A still small voice spake unto me,
"Life is so full of misery,
Were it not better not to be?"

Alfred Tennyson

Quatrain

A quatrain is a four-line stanza. The rhyme scheme is up to the writer. The first and third lines may rhyme, the second and fourth, all four rhyme: aa-bb; ab-ab; aaaa; abba; abbc; abcc; aabc; abca; etc.

What is the universe: What is the sky?
Where will I go on the day that I die?
If I walked through a mirror, what
would I find?
What is my body? What is my mind?

Diane McConkey
Age thirteen

The rain is good to us,
It rains on people on the bus.
It rains on farmer's crops.
It seems to me it never stops.

Jerry
Age nine

Cinquain

A cinquain is a stanza or a poem of five lines. Any rhyme scheme.

Sestet

A sestet is a stanza or a poem of six lines. Any rhyme scheme.

HUMOROUS POETRY

Any poem can be funny, of course, but several forms are traditionally used for humor. These are all rhymed.

The Limerick

Children like these funny poems. The form is five lines with aabba rhyme scheme. Have class clap the rhythm before attempting to write it.

There was an old soldier of Blister
Went walking one day with his sister,
When a cow at one poke
Tossed her into an oak,
Before the old gentleman missed her.

Mother Goose

There once was a child so light,
He could float to an incredible height.
He went out one day,
The wind blew him away,
And now he howls on an endless flight.

Danny Reich
Age thirteen

The Clerihew

Named after its inventor, Edmond Clerihew Bentley (1875-1956), the clerihew is a humorous poem of four lines. Often it is a mini-biography. The rhyme is aabb.

> *Old Andy Jackson*
> *Was half Anglo-Saxon.*
> *He was so full of beans*
> *That he took New Orleans.*

> *Eleanor Roosevelt*
> *Regardless of how she felt*
> *Traveled around the world*
> *Keeping our flag unfurled.*

Rhymed Daffynitions

> *"Walking"*
>
> *Our best hunch*
> *for the energy crunch.*

Scotch Jingles

> *The conductor called*
> *from the space ship station,*
> *"All aboard for*
> *the alienation!"*

POETRY WITH A SHAPE

Some poetry can be arranged on the page in any shape that the writer desires. Perhaps the shape fits the subject of the poem. "Song of the Decanter" by Warfield Creath Richardson is arranged in the shape of a vase or urn. Light verse is often written in very creative shapes, even in a circle.

ABC Poetry

One line is written per letter of the alphabet. You may start at any place. Poems may be as long as the child desires.

Baseballers
 Catch
  Dang
   Endless
    Flies,
     Good
      Hot dogs
       Into
        Jumping
         Kids
          Like
           Myself

Steve Branstetter
Age thirteen

No
 One
  Politely
   Quiets
    Restless
     Spectators

Steve
Age thirteen

Queens
 Race
  Staggering
   Turtles
    Uphill

Margie
Age nine

Ravens
 Start
  Trick-or-treating
   Until
    Vultures
     Wait

Margie McIntosh
Age nine

Diamente

This form of poem comes out shaped like a diamond so some children call them diamond poems.

one word—subject (noun)
two words—adjectives; describes subject
three words—participles, tell about subject
four words—nouns relating to subject
  (two may relate to top word, two to
  bottom)
three words—participles, tell about
  opposite word
two words—adjectives, describe opposite word
one word—noun, opposite of subject

birds
soft delicate
peeping, chirping, talking
sparrows, robins, swallows, blue jays
flying soaring, swooping
big, beautiful
eagle

Dea Hynes
Age fourteen

friend
nice, fun
laughing, playing, remembered
love, kindness, forgiveness, caring
crying, fighting, hating
mean, boring
enemy

Johanna
Age ten

winter
crisp, cold
snowing, raining, hiding
snowmen, firelight, storms, games
warming, melting, thawing
sunlight, fresh air
spring

Dea Hynes
Age fourteen

sneakers
dirty, smelling
weathered, sneaking, striped
size two-and-a-half, leather, laces, rubber
sticking, chewed, disgusting
yucky, gooey
gum

Danny Reich
Age ten

cages
iron, cold
small, dirty, musty
black, disappointment, crying, sadness
fresh, snow, cool
peaceful, enjoyment
wild

Krista
Age eleven

Creative Assignment

Take a Mother Goose Nursery Rhyme and write it in several styles of poetry.

Little Miss Muffet
Sat on a tuffet
Eating her curds and whey.
Along came a spider
Sat down beside her
And frightened Miss Muffet away.

Mother Goose

There once was a spider named Snider,
Who attempted to share apple cider.
But he scared Miss Muffet
While she sat on her tuffet
And she spilled the cider beside her.

Little Miss Muffet
Sat around on a tuffet
Eating curds and whey
Throughout all the day.

Stay, golden spider
Floating on your silken thread.
Frightened, the poor child.

No wonder that spider.
Sat down beside her.
It comes as no surprise
That she needed exercise.

spider
leggy, furry
floating, sailing, spinning
arachnid, creature, cocoon, web
screaming, running, fleeing
frightened, Muffet
girl

Quiet
  Resting
    Spider
      Turns
        Up
          Vocal
            Waif

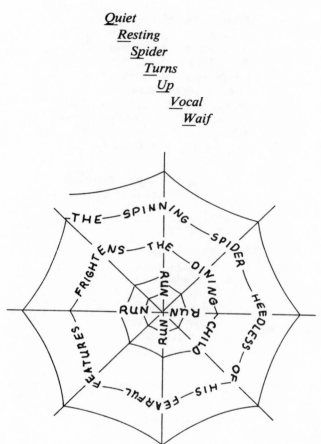

POEMS WITH RHYTHM

Mother Goose rhymes are popular because of their rhythm. Children love to memorize poetry with rhyme and rhythm and will chant along with you as you read familiar poems. Let children jump to poems, even jump rope as you read. Then they can try writing poems of their own that have lots of rhythm.

How do you do, sir?
How are you, sir?
Your leg has gone lame, sir?
Why that's a shame, sir.
I hope you feel better, sir,
That's a very nice sweater, sir.
Well, I must say good day, sir.
I'll be on my way, sir.
Well, yes, I'd like to stay, sir.
But, frankly, you haven't
much to say, sir.

Kiersten Remmers
Age thirteen

"Gay Time"

The gay time,
Is school time,
And school time,
Is in day time.
So all of you
Have a gay time,
In school time,
In the day time.

Jerry
Age nine

Creative Assignment

Take a jump rope rhyme and rewrite it for a poem of your own.

Down by the river
Where the green grass grows,
There sat Mary
As sweet as a rose.
She sang, she sang,
She sang so sweet.
Along came Billy
And kissed her on the cheek.
(How many kisses did he give her?)

Out in the orchard
    Where the apple trees grow,
A robin perched,
    Unaware of the snow.
He sang his song
    We love to hear:
Spring is coming,
    Have no fear.

SOUND WORD POETRY

Poems that use sound words to describe a scene or happening are fun to read and write. Go back to the chapter on words and talk about sound words. Try to write poems where the word echoes the sounds heard.

"The Squirrel"

Whisky, frisky
Hippity hop,
Up he goes
To the tree top!
Whirly, twirly,
Round and round
Down he scampers
To the ground.

Furly, curly
What a tail!
Tall as a feather
Broad as a sail!
Where's his supper?
In the shell.
Snappity, crackity
Out it fell.

Anonymous

"Heart Rhythms"

My heart beats slow,
Boomp, boomp, boomp, boomp.
My heart beats fast,
Bump, bump, bump, bump, bump.

Heather Aker
Age ten

Children who have written a lot of poems will probably enjoy poetry all of their lives. Rhythm is such a natural part of life. Rhyming is fun and is an essential tool for teaching reading skills. A life filled with poetry is a life enriched.

> *Poetry is a flock of seagulls*
> *over the ocean.*
> *Poetry is the pounding wave*
> *on a sandy shore.*
> *Poetry is the stillness*
> *of a calm summer day.*
> *Poetry is the laughter*
> *of falling in the sand.*
> *Poetry is racing to the water*
> *with your brother.*
> *Everything is poetry.*
>
> Rick Wehner
> Age eleven

SHARING POETRY

All poetry writing sessions should be followed by enjoyment of the finished products. After all, poetry is written to be read aloud. Let children share their own poems, read aloud each other's poems. Let children record their poems and then make the recordings available in the Poetry Corner. Make up slide shows or overhead projector shows where pictures illustrate class poems. Perhaps some poems could be set to music and sung in a class program. Share and enjoy.

TEACHING AND EVALUATING

Teaching poetry writing is a subtle art. Perhaps the most successful method is to: 1. Introduce the form, if any is to be used. 2. Read many examples, not being concerned with imitation. Read both adult poets and examples written by children. 3. Share children's attempts and praise originality. Point out individual improvement.

Do not grade poems. Use these suggestions to evaluate the work done:

1. Does this poem show any originality? Has the writer looked at his world in a new or different way? Expressed an emotion?

2. Has the writer used the best words—words that do justice to his ideas?

3. Does the poem paint a picture?

4. Has the writer developed the images he has introduced?

5. Has the writer tried so hard to rhyme that he has changed or lost the meaning of the poem?

6. What has writing the poem done for the child who wrote it?

There is a step from there [the physical act of writing] to the understanding that they are saying something when they write. The important thing at this point is not to feed writing to the child as you feed worms to a young robin. Writing should not be stuffing, but evoking.

I go habitually to fourth and fifth grades with poems written by other children of the same age, which poems I read to the class for about fifteen minutes. By this time you can see they are saying, "Oh, gee, I can do that."

And so they do.

Florence Becker Lennon
American poet

eleven

Children and Journal Keeping

I'll call for pen and ink and write my mind.

I'll call for pen and ink and write my mind.

Shakespeare,
Henry VI

Journal keeping: private and personal are the key words.

"I thought this class was very interesting and the journal was more fun than the one I did in school." Jackie, age thirteen, on her evaluation sheet.

In talking to children about the journals they had previously kept, we found that the ones they had written in school had to be turned in and read by the teacher for their grade.

"We kept a journal in junior high," a young woman said at a workshop. "But I never wrote my real feelings down because I knew the teacher would take it up and read it. I just made up stuff."

Others do the same thing, writing either very esoteric prose or details about events that they hope will shock the reader. Fantasy it is — journal keeping it is not.

Journal keeping for a class has to be an optional activity. Then the child has to know no one will read his journal unless he volunteers to share. He is invited to share something with the class or the teacher but only in his own time. A teacher can encourage sharing after building a level of trust with the children. There might be a secret drawer in the teacher's desk where journals could be placed for sharing with teacher only. Or a child could select something to read aloud to the teacher privately, to a small group, or to the class.

Some writing is too personal to share. But we need to write down our secrets. Cecily, in Oscar Wilde's *The Importance of Being Earnest*, says, "I keep a diary in order to enter the wonderful secrets of my life. If I didn't write them down I would probably forget all about them." It is a great joy in later life to remember the secrets and dreams of our youth.

We would not think of entering another person's home without knocking, going into a friend's room, poking around. Why do we try to enter a child's secret life without being invited? We have our students title their record books, "The Secret Journal of Mark Jones." By placing the word *secret* on the book we are all agreeing to a privacy pact.

Journals can take several forms. A spiral notebook eight and a half by eleven inches or nine and a half by six inches is one of the best choices for children. There are actual hard-bound books with blank pages, but these are scary to use at first. We have carefully trained children not to write in textbooks, so it's not easy to write freely in this clean, bound book. Discourage the lined, dated diaries that as children we started so religiously every January first. So little space in which to write each day is limiting, and we feel guilty when we don't write.

There is also a difference between a journal and a diary. A diary is used for the logging in of daily events. Sometimes that takes five lines, sometimes one, sometimes ten. And many days there is no time or there is nothing one cares to note. Journal entries can go back in time and forward into the future as well as record daily events and our thoughts about them.

Creative Assignment

Keep a dialogue journal between child and teacher. Each journal is a private correspondence for just the two people. At first the writing may consist of only a few lines, a question or two, a thought about the other person. As the trust and interest grow, some students will write a page or two, working out problems that are difficult to share face to face, thinking on paper, sharing thoughts, dreams, and philosophy, or merely interests and favorite things. The journal may go back and forth weekly or on whatever schedule the teacher can handle. Time consuming? Yes, but insightful. You will know your students better than you ever have, and they will get to know you as a person.

Writing in any journal should be spontaneous and done according to the individual's time preference. It can be compared to visiting with a friend. Sometimes we visit every day, sometimes we go a week without writing. Habit is a factor, however. And writing is something we need to make time for. If one waits for extra time, it may be never, another "something I'd like to do someday." Just fifteen minutes a day before we go to bed at night, when we wake in the morning, while we eat lunch, stolen moments from a busy schedule. Children today are just as scheduled as adults. Teach them to steal private moments from a day.

The friend we are visiting is oneself. And in these conversations we get to know ourselves better. Developing language skills is a purpose of any kind of writing. But the main purpose of keeping a journal is keeping in touch with that person inside, the secret person behind the public person.

CONTENTS OF A JOURNAL

What goes in journals? Anything children want. Their journals belong to them. What they write, how they write it, is up to them. They can write sideways, backwards, mirror writing, in a circle, in code. They can draw pictures. They can paste in cartoons or clippings of any kind. Not so that it turns into a scrapbook, but all of us have seen cartoons that spoke to us, sometimes illustrated the kind of day we'd had. This kind of personal clipping and recording is the one to encourage.

There are some basic content areas that we can suggest:

Feelings

Thoughts

Experiences

Things you hear

Things you see

Your favorite things

Your favorite sounds, sights, smells, things heard or touched

Ideas you have

Things that make you laugh, cry, get angry

Lists of any kind

Things you want to do

Your own poems

Poems you like that someone else wrote

Your own stories

Pieces of writing you like

Dreams

Fantasies

Dates you want to remember

Things you want to forget

Even though the journal belongs to the child, and she can write what she likes, suggestions from the teacher are helpful. A journal assignment each week (remember, not to be handed in, trust her to write it—or not write it if she chooses) establishes habit and may draw interesting things from a child, perceptive peeks into her personality.

(There is one journal rule. Record the date every time you write.)

Here are some of our suggestions for children writing in journals:

I wish....

I used to think....

If I had three wishes, they would be....

I get so angry when....

I'd like to be _____ when I grow up and here's why....

The funniest thing that ever happened to me was....

The scariest thing that ever happened to me was.... And here's what I did about it....

My most embarrassing moment was _____ and here's how I felt about it....

If I could be any animal, I'd be a _____ because....

If I could go back in time, I'd go to _____ (date) because....

Here are some things I'd do while I was back in time....

If I could go forward in time, I'd see _____ or do _____

A story about my going back or forward in time....

If I could be anyone else in the whole world today, it would be _____ because _____ and here's what my life would be like....

If I had a million dollars, I'd....

If I was in charge of the whole world, I'd....

If I could change three things in my life, they'd be....

These are joys in my life....

I believe.... I don't believe....

One night I dreamed....

Sometimes I don't understand....

Sometimes I wonder about....

Sometimes I'm lonely when....

My poem about being lonely....

Here's what I do best....

Write a recipe of yourself. Be sure and give the mixing directions.

"Recipe of Myself"

2 Tbsp. Smart Alec
2 Cups Action
Dash Intellect
1 Cup Leadership
5 oz. Guts
5 Leaves Hot Temper

Mix leadership with hot temper with electric blender on high speed. Set aside. Preheat oven to 250°. Mix all ingreedy-ents with spoon until slightly lumpy. Pour into 15x24x3 pan (greased) and cook until golden grown. Then remove and pour other ingreedy-ents over for icing.

Ben
Age twelve

Here's how I feel about being alone sometimes....

Lonely sounds, things that make me think of loneliness....

My favorite book is _____ and I like it because....

My favorite TV show is _____ and I like it because....

My favorite movie is _____ and I liked it because....

Someday I'd like to write....

I like to write because....

Here's how I feel when I'm writing....

The most amazing thing I ever saw was....

I don't understand _____ about myself and here's how I feel about that....

My favorite color is _____ . Here's how that color makes me feel....

My favorite weather is _____ because.... Here's how I feel during that kind of weather....

If I could live any place in the world, I'd live in _____ because....

Here's how it looks outside my window when I live there....

My dream house is....

Here's what I think about God ... death ... divorce ... happiness ... friendship....

Here's what I think about myself as a person....

I wonder how others see me? I think....

Here's what makes me jump for joy....

Here's how I feel when I'm happy....

I have this dream....

Here's who I care about in my life _____ because....

What I enjoy most about school is....

What I enjoy least about school is....

My favorite teacher of all times is _____ because....

I liked being in his/her class because....

I like to learn new things because....

I think it would be fun to learn....

If I were marooned on a desert island, here's what I'd want with me.... And I'd want these three books....

If I were lost in the woods, here's what I'd do....

My life would be different if....

Here's who my friends are _____. I like them because....

The kind of people I like are....

Write a letter to: Dear Person way down inside me,
                   Dear Body,
                   Dear Mother,
                   Dear Father,
                   Dear Sister or Brother,
                   Dear Friend,
                   Dear Teacher,
                   Dear (pet),
                   Dear God,
                   Dear World,

Write a dialogue or conversation with the above people. This is different because they get to talk back.

Write a letter to someone you don't like.

Write a conversation with someone you don't like.

Pretend you are someone you hate. Write a story about your life.

Pretend you are someone in your family. Write a story about your life.

Journal keeping can play a very important part in a child's life. It can become a place to vent anger, explore inner feelings, get to know himself and other people. Giving a problem enough thought to be able to express it in writing can help in understanding and working out that problem. The writer gains perspective about feelings and thoughts by writing them down. This type of introspection can help a child grow emotionally, and also in the ability for creative expression. He can write freely most of the time because he is writing about familiar things, himself, the people around him. He doesn't worry about what someone else will think about the way he expresses himself, because no one else is ever going to see his efforts. This gives him a very free feeling towards writing.

The journal gives the creative child who loves to write a place to practice. He will develop a natural writing style, find his own voice. How nice it would have been to practice piano in private, hit the sour notes on a violin while alone so no one could hear.

Learning in public is very restricting, embarrassing, and sometimes painful. In her diary, Anne Frank said, "Paper is more patient than man." Giving children a private place to experiment and get to know themselves is a gift we can give them—one that will last a lifetime.

twelve

Revision

**Good stories are not written,
they are _re_written.**

Good stories are not written. They are rewritten.

Phyllis Whitney,
Writing Juvenile Fiction

The dictionary definition of *communicate* is to give or interchange thoughts, feelings, information, or the like, by writing, speaking, and so forth. If writing is to be communication—a sharing of thoughts, feelings, and information—then we should observe certain conventions of written communication. As writers we cheat ourselves as well as our would-be readers if we don't put our ideas down in a way that is both readable and understandable.

Children should be encouraged, not just to write, but to rewrite until it *is* right—not necessarily that it is *correct* in the eyes of others, but that it feels right to the writer.

While writing, writers must be subjective. They must be personally involved. We might say that they can't see the trees for the forest—or the bricks because they are looking at the wall. It is up to the editor to examine the bricks and decide if they are sound and then to help writers learn to be their own inspectors. Our analogy ends there, however, because criticism of someone's writing is a lot more like criticizing his family than like criticizing his bricks. While the editor's task is to see that writers write to the best of their ability, the editor has to do it in a helpful, encouraging, and tactful way.

May Sarton says, "An artist has to face awkwardness and failure in the very process of making his talent grow."[1] It is the teacher-editor's job to help the student-writer accomplish this growth. The teacher guides the student; first students work with teacher as editor, next with peers as editors, and then by themselves as their own editors. Student writers learn to use the checklist questions that will help them evaluate their work, to understand the difference between *rewriting* and *copying over*, and, finally, to enjoy the pleasure of communicating their own thoughts and ideas to classmates and friends. Following a piece of writing from rough draft through to final revision gives teachers an idea of what children are capable of, and gives children confidence in what they can accomplish.

The authors wish to thank Noel Pazour for his contributions to the material in this chapter.

THREE TYPES OF EDITING

One of the aims of classroom writing is to help children become their own editors—that is, to look at their own writing objectively, and to become independent and responsible for their own writing. We reach this goal through the steps of teacher-editing to peer-editing and peer-editing to self-editing.

Teacher-editing

In the beginning the teacher will be the editor. Since the teacher is the model for the kind of editors the children become, teachers should keep several guidelines in mind, always remembering Mauree Applegate's statement in her book, *Freeing Children to Write*:

> A child's story should never be evaluated apart from the child who wrote it.[2]

First, don't forget the importance of mutual TRUST.

Second, teach the children that criticism should be KNOWLEDGEABLE AND THOUGHTFUL EVALUATION, not just faultfinding and censure.

Third, remember that in order to be helpful, criticism should be given in a POSITIVE way. Writing teachers, including those who work with adults, do far more harm than good when they tear stories to shreds, disparage and put down students. Such teachers are displaying their own inadequacies. The teacher who gets good results is the one who finds something to commend and works from there.

Which brings us to point

Four, PRAISE. Praise builds incentive. Too little praise may result in discouragement. Too much praise, when the child knows it isn't deserved, creates confusion and distrust. Or, it can cause the child to work for praise instead of working to find his own ideas and thoughts. Honest, deserved praise gives a feeling of accomplishment and encouragement.

Fifth, remain OBJECTIVE. The editor does not attempt to rewrite the story *his* way. This is someone else's story, someone else's idea. (If the editor thinks it should be done another way, let him write his own story.)

Sixth, FORGET ABOUT SPELLING AND GRAMMAR RULES FOR A WHILE. The first draft of any writing is spontaneous. It mustn't get bogged down by mechanics. (Remember, ideas often come faster than young children can write.) We've all read in the Dear Abby or Ann Landers columns about people who have had their letters returned, by friends or family, corrected like English themes.

Their reactions have been, *You aren't listening to me. You don't care about what I'm trying to say.* After all, WHAT is being said is here more important than HOW it is being said. Ronald L. Cramer warns, "Teachers should accept children's early misspellings in the same spirit that parents accept the early mispronunciation in children's oral language."[3] And Mauree Applegate reminds us that the most intriguing words are the hardest to spell.[4]

Seventh, THE FIRST DRAFT IS JUST THE BEGINNING. Except for journal notes or very personal writing where little or no editing should be done, a child shouldn't feel that the first draft is the final draft. Some may insist they can't do better — either because they *doubt* their own ability or because they *overestimate* their own ability. But if you were teaching clothing design and construction, you would never accept a garment as completed while it was still held together by pins. Think of the first draft as ideas that have been pinned together. Editing and revision (trying on and fitting?) are a basic part of writing. They are not to be confused with "copying over."

Checklists

Someone has suggested that the word *revision* be thought of as RE-VISION — seeing again. This is what the teacher-editor helps the child-writer to do: to look at his writing again, to see it as others would see it.

The first questions the editor asks are:

What is it the writer wants to say? What is his idea?

Has he said it?

and then

Has she said it clearly?

Has he arranged what he is telling in the best order?

Has she omitted any important details?

Has he repeated details unnecessarily?

Has she used the best words?

Should she use more words? Fewer words?

Has he caught our attention with a good beginning?

Has he held our interest through the middle part?

Has he given us a satisfactory ending?

and for fiction

Is the plot carefully worked out?

Is anything told too soon, spoiling the suspense?

Is there conversation?

Is there description?

Is there character development?

Remember, too, the basic WHO, WHAT, WHEN, WHERE, WHY, and HOW? These six questions are as applicable to fiction as they are to nonfiction.

Plot is WHAT happens, HOW it happens.
Characters are to WHOM it happens.
Setting is WHERE and WHEN it happens.
And WHY it happens is the theme or premise of the story.

After looking at the written piece as a whole, check paragraphs, sentences, and individual words.

Paragraphs   Are they clear?
                Does each one help to tell the story?

Sentences   Are they clear?
                Are they in logical order to make an understandable paragraph?
                Are they varied in type and length?

Words   Are they used correctly?
                Do they help our imaginations see, hear, smell, taste, touch?
                Do they help us feel emotions?

The Conference

When children's ideas are good they must be told so. Children sense that content and ideas are more fundamental to good writing than are mechanics. When children know their ideas are good they will learn the mechanics of writing more readily.

Ronald Cramer[5]

Now of course you're not going to throw all of this to the child at once. That would overwhelm any writer. You'll be asking the questions as you read the story to yourself. When you are ready to talk with the writer, you'll reword the applicable questions to discuss with him.

To begin with, find something good to praise; then talk about the questions you've chosen; finally, choose some weak points to begin reworking. These might be the weaknesses most glaringly in need of correction, or, depending on the child, they may be points that he can improve easily without getting too discouraged. But always keep in mind that fundamental question, "*What do you want to say*?"

Encourage the writer by using open-ended questions, especially with praise for whatever can be praised, instead of a blunt, "This is the way to do it."

"This sentence is good. Now how can we make *this* sentence stronger?"

"When you say *shivery with excitement* here, I understand just how you feel. But over here, when you say *he's a good guy*, GOOD doesn't make me see him or feel I know this fellow the way you do. What are some other words?..."

Editing Workshops

The teacher-as-editor will also conduct editing workshops. These can begin with discussions of strong and weak points common among all the students—a session on incomplete sentences, perhaps, with made-up examples or unidentified sentences taken from actual work for demonstration.

After the writers have developed some self-confidence the workshop can move on to identified work for discussion, especially to illustrate strong points and good examples.

One workshop session might be on ways to begin stories, using the children's own writing as well as books and stories they are reading. They could find and bring examples of different kinds of story and article openings:

action
description of a place or person
conversation
a question
a startling statement
an anecdote

A workshop on writing more interesting sentences could include exercises in expanding words, phrases, and sentences. See the section "Sensory Awareness" in chapter 5 and the section "Putting Words to Work" in chapter 7.

Read to the children and have them read aloud from examples of excellent writing. The natural pauses, inflections, and rhythms will develop a feeling for well-written sentences. Or, reverse the process. Have them read aloud paragraphs in which all capitalization and punctuation have been removed. They will discover how important details are for understanding.

As they become more self-confident, use identified portions of their writings for discussing ways of improvement—writing conversations, developing mood, creating suspense.

Peer-editing

Have children read their writing aloud to each other. When they are ready to read to their classmates they are ready for the step to peer-editing. This works best in small groups, with the children reading each other's stories, listening to them being read aloud, and then discussing what they like, what they feel can be improved. They should use the checklists in their groups the way they have learned to use them with the teacher as editor.

Self-editing

Peer-group editing moves gradually into self-editing. Encourage children to read their writing aloud (even if there is no one else around to listen) in order to hear what it sounds like. The ear catches rough places that the eye can miss. The tape recorder can be an effective tool in helping children hear their own writing more objectively. At any rate, students should listen to their stories, then work through them, examining paragraphs, sentences, words, asking themselves the checklist questions.

Self-editing does not mean giving up peer-editing, and peer-editing does not mean the end of teacher-editing. They can all supplement and complement each other.

REWRITING

Improving Design and Improving Communication

The second step of revision is rewriting. There are two goals here:

1. **Improving design**—the overall impression of the piece. (Have I said what I want to say?)

2. **Improving communication**—the technical or mechanical structure of the piece: wording, sentence structure, sentence and paragraph order and sequence. (Have I said it so the reader can understand?)

The writer writes the story again—and perhaps again and again. Here the teacher must use judgment as to how much time a child should spend on one piece. Too much rewriting can take the spontaneity and style out of any story. The writing might be good enough that minor changes will suffice, or it might be a piece that doesn't warrant a great deal of time and effort. A long story that a child is really excited about might deserve several weeks of work.

Other Kinds of Rewriting

Students may be interested in experimenting with other forms of rewriting, also:

Fiction
> Put the story characters in a new setting or situation, a sequel.
>
> Put new characters in the old setting or situation.
>
> Write an alternate ending.
>
> Rewrite the story as a play.

Poetry and Nonfiction
> Change prose into poetry.
>
> Change poetry into prose.
>
> Put the piece into a letter to a real, imaginary, historical, or fictional character.
>
> Rewrite as a news or feature story for a newspaper.

A Works-in-Progress portfolio is a good idea. Setting something aside for a time and coming back to it later with a more objective eye is a requisite of self-editing. Completed manuscripts that might be used for experimental writing can be kept in the portfolio, too.

COPYEDITING AND PROOFREADING

When the child feels he has done the best he can with his rewriting, when he is reasonably satisfied, then it is time for the third step. This is copyediting and proofreading. Technically, proofreading is the final checking of a printer's proof for typographical errors, and copyediting is the correcting of copy for errors in style, spelling, punctuation, and grammar. While the term proofreading is often used to cover both, this step of the revision process is the copyeditor's job. And, of course, writers must become the very best copyeditors they are capable of being.

A writer asks, reading a story still another time,

Have I checked the spelling of all the words?

Have I punctuated correctly?

Have I capitalized all the words that should be capitalized?

Have I written and placed the title in the proper way?

Have I made proper margins and indentations for paragraphs?

When writers are sure their manuscripts pass these first questions on the list, then it is time to copy them, asking themselves the last question as they do so:

Am I writing neatly and carefully so that my manuscript will be easy for others to read?

After copying a manuscript, the writer reads it once more, proofreading a last time for misspellings or omitted words.

The goal of classroom editing is not perfection. The goal is to present interesting thoughts, exciting ideas, imaginative plots, in the best possible way: told with attention-holding words, written in understandable, grammatical form, and copied in readable handwriting, typescript, or print-out. *The goal is the sharing of expression.*

NOTES

1.   May Sarton, *House by the Sea* (New York: W. W. Norton and Co., Inc., copyright 1977 by May Sarton), 82.

2.   Mauree Applegate, *Freeing Children to Write* (New York: Harper & Row, 1963), 96.

3.   Ronald Cramer, *Writing, Reading, and Language Growth* (Columbus, Ohio: Charles E. Merrill Publishing Co., 1978), 107.

4.   Applegate, *Freeing Children to Write*, 77.

5.   Cramer, *Writing, Reading, and Language Growth*, 84.

Appendix A

A Why? Who? When and Where?
What? and How?
of
Creative Writing Projects
for Children

Are you interested in a creative writing project for children? A Writers' Workshop, a Book Festival, a Conference for Young Writers? Who would take part in your program? When and where would it be held? Who would direct it? Who would sponsor it?

These and other questions on the following pages are all to be considered and answered before organizing a children's writing project. Several plans are described and a sample kit for organizing one type of project is included. The questions, ideas, and examples are not meant as a set of rules for carrying out a program. They are a collection of suggestions that we have seen actually used, productively and successfully carried out, in creative writing programs, conferences, and workshops.

WHY?

challenge....participation...
...sharing....achievement...

In chapter 1 we presented our own answers, as well as some answers from other teachers and writers, to the question, "Why write?" The reasons most often given for encouraging children to write are these four:

1. Writing gives children the opportunity to express and share their own thoughts and ideas.

2. It develops competence.

3. It can be therapy for the children and also give us adults insights to their problems and needs.

4. It encourages and develops creativity.

These are valid answers to the question, "Why write?" but why should we go to all the work of having a writing project, a workshop, or a conference for children?

It is frequently remarked that writing is a lonely business. And another remark, just as frequently heard at adult writers' workshops and conferences, is, "It's wonderful to find other people who are interested in writing—now I don't feel so alone."

Writers (unless involved with a cooperative project) must work alone. But to be working in a community of writers, close to others interested in the same achievements and goals, gives stimulation, encouragement, and inspiration. This surely is just as true for children who want to write as it is for adults. And beginners deserve all the help they can get.

Learning at an early age to put one's thoughts down on paper can develop more than just a capable writer. It will, of course, make the writing process easier as the writer grows older, but it may also open other doors that are not so easily opened later on.

It is often said that we are a nation of spectators. We may be participating vicariously, but we probably spend very little of our leisure time in some sort of active participation. The more opportunities children have to participate in a variety of creative activities, the more interest and capability they will develop and carry with them into their adulthood. So our answer to the question, "Why write?" is

> Taking part in a writing project gives children the challenge of creating and accomplishing; of conceiving, planning, and carrying out an idea; and of discovering for themselves the pleasure, the satisfaction, *the joy of writing.*

WHO?

selected children....all grades...
....school-sponsored...club- or library-sponsored....

Who will participate in your children's writing project?

Will it be an elementary and middle school project? Will it be open to junior and senior high school students as well? Will every child who is interested be able to take part? (Not all children want to write.) Or will the workshop or conference be for selected children? Perhaps you will want to start modestly with a single-classroom workshop. There will always be room and time to grow. One very successful annual conference now includes the entire school district.

Who will sponsor your project?

Will it be a class endeavor carried out by the teacher? A grade-level project? Will all upper grades in one school take part? Or in the entire district? Will it be directed by a school-involved organization such as a parent-teacher group or an educational association? Will the city library conduct a workshop? Or would a private organization such as a writers' club or service or educational sorority or fraternity undertake it? To what extent would these groups be able or willing to help finance the project?

WHEN AND WHERE?

after school...summer vacation....
....Children's Book Week....
classroom....public library...

Will the project be a school-time activity? Curriculum-related? An after-school or released-time workshop?

Will it be an autumn kick-off, a part of Children's Book Week, a Book Fair, or Festival celebration? Or will it be an activity for summer vacation?

Will it take place within the school, at a library, a community center? Or will it be a small group meeting in someone's home?

How long will the workshop last? One day? Over a period of several weeks? Will there be a culminating celebration when books or manuscripts are displayed for visitors, with recognition for all participants? With, perhaps, professional writers, librarians, story-tellers as special guests? Will there be punch and cookies? Young writers always need nourishment.

WHAT?

workshop...conference...short term....
....continuing project....

Following are descriptions of five types of workshops which the authors have observed or participated in. The first four are described briefly; plans and procedures for the fifth are given in detail.

It is very important to be aware that the workshops and conferences included here *are not contests*. There are no prizes, first places, blue ribbons, Oscars, Pulitzers, or even Best of Show. If any sort of awards are given — certificates or other mementos — *they are given to every child who participates*.

A Half-day, One-grade Workshop

One type of school-related workshop is presented on half of a school day for selected children from a single grade level. Participants are chosen on a basis of interest indicated by writing they have done during the year. Each child submits a sample of his writing (fiction or nonfiction, poetry or prose), and these are distributed to area authors or teachers who lead the workshop. A written critique is returned to each child with his manuscript during the meeting. First, all the students hear the authors or an illustrator or librarian speak on various aspects of writing and producing books. They then divide into small groups with the authors who have read their manuscripts for a period of discussion, writing, idea-getting, and questions. The half-day ends with a question and answer period for all, and a social time: punch, cookies, and visiting.

The workshop these authors have taken part in for several years has half a dozen writer-leaders, each meeting with about a dozen fifth-graders at three half-day workshops. This involves over two hundred children from throughout the school district. When those children return to their own classrooms they present what they have learned in the workshop to their peers. Whether or not this kind of project helps the entire class depends entirely on the teacher's involvement and cooperation, both before and after the workshop. Writing and discussion workshops for teachers at the beginning of the year have proved helpful in developing understanding and interest about the children's workshops.

A Non-school, One-month Workshop

A second project, "Adventures in Writing," presents a non-school-related afternoon workshop for all interested children of fourth, fifth, and sixth grades. Meeting with the children at the public library, members of a local writers' club, sponsors of the workshop, each speak briefly about getting ideas, doing research, illustrating, writing short stories, articles, plays, and poetry. "How-to" booklets prepared by the club are given to all the children, and they are encouraged to write and enter a piece for an anthology to be compiled by the club. Given a one-month deadline, the children have another opportunity to meet with the authors for help and discussion at the half-way point. At the end of the month the sponsors prepare the manuscripts for a printed booklet. Then the participating children and their parents are invited to an afternoon party at the library where the children are introduced and presented with copies of the book. Since this workshop is conducted by a private group, an entry fee to cover printing costs could be charged. An important detail to the children at any of these conferences or workshops is the social hour at the end, which gives them the time to visit, exchange autographs, and, to be sure, to have punch and cookies.

A Summer Listening-and-Writing Workshop

Another non-school, summer project, "Adventures in Listening, Experiments in Writing," is supported by grants from private organizations or from a municipal arts program. It is free to students finishing sixth grade, but enrollment is limited to twenty children for each two-weeks' workshop. The students meet twice a week. During the first three mornings they spend an hour listening to and discussing talks given by authorities on subjects as varied as archeological digs and living in the year A.D. 2000, grand opera and glaciers. The talk session is followed by an hour of writing and talking about writing techniques with a teacher who is a professional writer. While it is preferred that the children write—prose, poetry, news reports, letters, whatever they wish—on the subject they have just heard, that is not required. Their manuscripts are read by the instructor and returned at the next session, each with a page of comments and suggestions. The fourth morning of the workshop is spent in personal conferences for each participant with the writing instructor. An anthology including each writer's favorite pieces is published at the end of the workshop.

After School or Vacation Classes

These classes, ten hour-and-a-half sessions, are taught by a local children's book writer. Classes are limited to ten to fifteen students. Subjects are writing technique and poetry in the class called "Creative Writing" and techniques of short story writing in the class titled "Story Writing." Each class consists of presentation and discussion, a writing session, reading and sharing with the class, and teacher critique. Evaluation of work is aimed at "writing it better." Homework is given in the short story class with stories of different genre assigned. At the end of the class each student, with the help of the teacher, selects his best work to be included in a class publication. Because the classes are private instruction, a fee is charged.

HOW?

The following pages include illustrations and step-by-step plans for carrying out a children's writing conference.

**READ A BOOK-WRITE A BOOK
CONFERENCE KIT**

Philosophy of the READ A BOOK-WRITE A BOOK CONFERENCE

   I. Steps for organizer and coordinators

   II. Letter of explanation to all adults who might be interested in conference

  III. Packet for teachers:
     A. Letter to teachers
     B. Poster
     C. Letter for parents
     D. Writing tips
     E. Calendar
     F. Bookplate

Additional Material for Organizer and Coordinators:

   IV. Letter to teachers of high school writing classes

   V. Tips for critics

   VI. Critic's evaluation sheet

  VII. Letter to participating student-writers

  VIII. Letter to participating student-critics

   IX. Sample certificate

   X. Options

THE READ A BOOK-WRITE A BOOK CONFERENCE

We hope this kit will be of help to you. The Philosophy of the READ A BOOK-WRITE A BOOK CONFERENCE is that the pleasure of writing the book and the accomplishment of having written the book are their own rewards. If you use the name READ A BOOK-WRITE A BOOK CONFERENCE we do ask two things of you: First, that ideas or hopes of commercial publication never be used as incentive for your students, or even suggested; second, that all children participating receive equal recognition (public acknowledgment, certificates, mementos), and that there be no differentiating awards. A writing conference is not a contest. And whether you use this plan, something suggested by it, or an entirely different approach, we wish you success with your conference and much good reading and writing from your students.

I. STEPS FOR ORGANIZER AND COORDINATORS

1. Choose sponsor. (School, school-related organization, club or service fraternity, etc.)

2. Set date, time, and place.

3. Appoint and meet with coordinators for each school or group of schools.

4. Send letters of explanation about the conference to principals, supervisors, teachers, librarians, and writers who might be interested in participating.

5. Hold a kick-off meeting for teachers featuring a speaker who is enthusiastic about children's writing. (Schools and individual classrooms may want to hold their own kick-off meetings, too.)

6. Arrange for distribution of conference packets to participating teachers in their schools.

7. Invite local librarians, writers, and high school writing teachers to participate in conference, explaining what is wanted and expected of them. (Honorariums, travel expenses, sale of books, or any other questions should be settled at this time.) *Remind these guests of conference just before the day of conference.*

    Make sure that information about and books by the guests are made available in every classroom, and that all participants know something about the guests and, with authors, what they have written.

8. Calendar: Arrange dates and deadlines for and deliveries of

    letters to parents

    letters to teachers of high school writing classes

    completion of books

    books and evaluation sheets to high schools for criticism

    books to place of conference

    additional meetings

    publicity releases

    letters to participating student-writers

    letters to participating student-critics

9. Decide on method to identify, inventory, pack and deliver books to their various destinations.

10. Arrange for publicity.

11. Order and prepare certificates or other mementos.

12. Arrange for responsible adults—teachers, parents—to be at each conference display table and to supervise reading circles if held.

13. Plan conference program:

    > special speakers
    > reading circles
    > presentation of certificates
    > social hour
    > book sales

14. Write thank-you letters.

II. To be sent to principals, supervisors, teachers, librarians, and writers who might be interested in participating in the conference.

Dear _____ ,

_____ is sponsoring a READ A BOOK-WRITE A BOOK CONFERENCE, a writing project for all interested children in grades _____ to _____, to be held on _____ at _____.

The purpose of the conference is to give grade school students an opportunity to take part in a creative and tangible project in which every child is a winner: Each child will have his book looked at, read from, and discussed; each child will receive a certificate of participation; each child will have an opportunity to meet local librarians, teachers, and writers.

The students are to write books, illustrate them if they wish, and to put them together in an attractive way. These books will be read and criticized (following guidelines for constructive criticism) by senior high school writing classes.

On _____, all entries will be displayed by school and grade. In small groups of children and parents the student-writers will have a chance to read selections from their books and talk about them. Each group will have a supervising adult. Librarians, participating high school writing teachers, and area authors of children's books will be invited to take part in the conference and in the discussions. Authors may read selections from their own works, but they will be there especially to talk about the children's writings with them. At the conclusion of the reading circles each student-writer will be given written criticism and a certificate.

After the conference the young writers' books can be put on display in their own schools. An optional project is to make the books a part of the school library.

A kick-off meeting featuring _____ as guest speaker will be held on _____ at _____ . Teachers interested in participating in the conference will receive packets of plans, suggestions, and materials from their own school coordinators.

Sincerely yours,

_____
Conference Organizer

III. PACKET FOR TEACHERS
    A. Letter to teachers
    B. Poster
    C. Letter for parents
    D. Writing tips
    E. Calendar
    F. Bookplate

A.   Letter to elementary teachers from local sponsor/organizer

Dear teacher:

Here is your READ A BOOK-WRITE A BOOK CONFERENCE packet. Enclosed are

1.   an announcement to be posted for students to read

2.   a letter for parents to be copied and sent home (see calendar)

3.   *Writing Tips*—suggestions and helps for writers to be copied and given to each participating child

4.   Calendar of dates and deadlines

5.   Bookplates that can be copied for student use

Each book should include the following:

name of author
grade
teacher's name
school

Conference bookplates can be used for the above identification.

Members of the _____ High School creative writing classes will criticize the books. A written criticism of his or her book will be given to each student the day of the conference.

Please have your books ready to be picked up on _____.

_____
Conference Organizer

_____
School Coordinator

READ A BOOK–

WRITE A BOOK

invites

you

to write a book
All books will be
looked at-read from-talked about
at
the Read a Book-Write a Book Conference
by
young writers, parents, teachers
librarians and local writers
of books for children

DATE

PLACE

ask your teacher for details

Figure 1. A Read a Book-Write a Book Poster for Teachers to Post in Classrooms

C.   Letter for parents

Dear Parents:

_____ is inviting every student in your district (or school) to READ A BOOK-WRITE A BOOK! and to take part in a conference for young writers to be held Saturday, _____, from _____ to _____ at _____ School.

The students are to write books, illustrate them if they wish, and put them together in an attractive way. The work is to be done at school.

The books will be displayed and discussed at the conference, students and their parents will have the opportunity to talk with teachers, librarians, and local authors of children's books, and each participating child will receive a certificate and a written evaluation of his book prepared by the creative writing classes of _____ High School.

This is an opportunity for your children to have a challenging purpose for writing and for carrying out a creative project. We hope that you will encourage them to take part.

_____
Conference Organizer

_____
School Coordinator

D. TIPS ON WRITING YOUR BOOK

1. Write about something you know or can find out about and something that is interesting to you.

2. Write the kind of story or book you like to read.

3. Give your story a good plot: Plot equals a person plus his or her problem plus *what he or she does about it.*

4. It is usually best to have just one *main* character in a story.

5. Be sure the main character is one your readers will like.

6. Give your characters interesting names. Plain people have plain names. Funny people have funny names. Historical characters can have old-fashioned names, and characters who live in the future or in fantasy worlds can have made-up names. Think about what kind of a person your character is when you look for a name. Use a "Name the Baby" book.

7. Your first sentence should "grab" the reader.

8. Use colorful verbs. Which is better?

   He *ran* from the old house, or He *fled* from the old house.

   She *sat* in her chair, or She *slumped* in her chair.

9. Use more nouns and verbs than adjectives and adverbs. Create scenes with words.

   The cellar was dark and the air reeked of mildew. Cobwebs spliced the corners.

   The meadow danced with daffodils. Sunlight sparkled the dust motes while spiders spun and birds warbled.

10. Vary sentence length. Short sentences create suspense and speed up action. Long sentences build a thoughtful, quiet mood and slow down action.

11. Use active, not passive, voice.

    (active)   Janet *heard* the rock falling.

    (passive)   A falling rock *was heard* by Janet.

12. Don't tell how something happened. Show it.

    (telling)   *Mark felt bad when he made the last out.*

    (showing)   *Mark dropped the bat and stumbled back to the dugout. It couldn't be tears that blurred his vision because he was too old to cry. He didn't dare look at Sam and Larry.*

13. Use the five senses to make your story come alive. Tell how things look, feel, smell, taste, or sound.

14. Write the story as if it were happening to you. (But not necessarily in first person.) Put yourself in your main character's place. How would you feel? What would you do?

15. Write the first draft of your story without worrying about spelling or grammar. You can clean it up later — take out parts you don't like, put in new parts, find a better word, check spelling and punctuation, and copy it neatly. It is important to get your story down on paper while it is alive and exciting in your imagination.

16. Read your story aloud to catch errors. Your ears will hear mistakes or rough spots that your eyes skip over.

E. Sample calendar for elementary school teachers

TEACHERS' CALENDAR

September __	Kick-off meeting _____, featured speaker
September __	Teachers receive conference packet from school coordinator
September-March	Reading and writing experiences in classrooms
October 1	(Optional: classroom or school kick-off meeting)
October 1	Letters to parents
November-February	(Optional: bookbinding workshops)
January-March	Learn about professional guests (librarians, writing teachers, authors, booksellers who will attend conference) Read from authors' books
February 1	Books delivered to high school writing classes for criticism
February __	Student-writers receive letters inviting them and their parents to the March conference
March __	Conference

CONFERENCE

_____

Book title

_____

Author

_____

School

_____

Teacher

Figure 2. READ A BOOK-WRITE A BOOK Bookplate

ADDITIONAL MATERIAL
FOR
ORGANIZERS AND COORDINATORS

IV.   Letter to teachers of high school writing classes

V.   Tips for critics

VI.   Critic's evaluation sheet

VII.   Letter to participating student-writers

VIII.   Letter to participating student-critics

IX.   Sample certificate

X.   Options

IV. Letter to teachers of high school writing classes

Dear Teacher:

_____ is sponsoring an elementary school READ A BOOK-WRITE A BOOK CONFERENCE for children interested in writing. To add extra value to this project for grade school students we should like to have members of your writing classes read the books and write criticism of them.

The books will be presented by their writers at the conference on Saturday, _____, from _____ to _____ at _____ School. Parents, librarians, and local writers of children's books will be present. Each writer will receive a certificate of participation and a written evaluation of his or her book.

We hope you will be interested in having your classes take part in this project. For further details please call us at _____.

_____

Conference Organizer

V.   Tips for Critics

TIPS FOR CRITICS

Reading someone else's manuscript and helping to make it better will help you to evaluate and make your own work better.

1.   Be helpful to the writer—not scornful.

2.   Do not put the writer down if the story is not a masterpiece. It is the best he or she can do at this time. Be understanding. The writer wants to be helped, not hurt.

3.   Be honest but diplomatic. The writer is a sensitive person. Being harsh or blunt will not help. Even if a manuscript is poor there are some good things about it. Point these out. Start your criticism with what is good about the manuscript.

4.   Don't be too general. Saying a story plot is poorly developed or a character poorly drawn is not enough. Tell the writer how to portray a character better, how to make a scene come alive, how to use stronger or more descriptive words.

5.   Try to forget whether or not *you* like the story. Discuss it from a reader's viewpoint.

Thank you for your time and work in helping a fellow writer.

VI.   Suggested evaluation sheet

CRITIC'S EVALUATION SHEET

1.   Has the writer said what he or she wants to say

   clearly?

   in the best order?

   in an interesting way?

2.   Prose

   Is there a good beginning?

   Does the middle hold our interest?

   Is there a satisfactory ending?

Fiction

   Is the plot carefully worked out? (Plot consists of a main character, his or her problem, and what he or she does about it.)

   Is there conversation?

   Is there description?

   Is there character development?

3.   Poetry

   Does it reflect the writer's feelings, mood, ideas?

   Are rhyme (if used) and rhythm appropriate to the subject?

4.   Style

   Is word choice appropriate, varied, interesting?

   Do sentences show variety in structure?

5.   Mechanics

   punctuation and capitalization

   spelling

   legibility

   neatness

VII. Letter to participating student-writers

Dear _____ ,

Congratulations for submitting a manuscript to the READ A BOOK-WRITE A BOOK CONFERENCE. You and your parents are invited to attend the conference on Saturday, _____, from _____ to _____ at _____ School.

At this time your book and the books of other student-writers from your school district will be on display, and you will receive a special certificate of participation from ____(sponsor)____.

You will also have the opportunity to discuss your writing with other young writers; meet professional authors including _____, _____, and _____; attend discussion sessions with them; and have your books autographed. The professional authors will be available all morning for you to meet personally.

We look forward to seeing you and your parents at this very special event.

Sincerely yours,

_____

Conference Organizer

VIII.   Letter to participating student-critics

Dear _____ ,

Thank you for your participation in our READ A BOOK-WRITE A BOOK CONFERENCE. All of the student-written books will be on display at the Saturday Conference on _____, from _____ to _____ at _____ School.

You are cordially invited to attend, see the books, and personally meet both the student-writers and the professional writers, _____, _____, and _____, who will also be guests.

We are looking forward to seeing you at the conference. Thank you again for your help.

Sincerely yours,

_____

Conference Organizer

YOUNG WRITERS' CONFERENCE

State of Colorado

This Certifies That _____

has written and presented a book for the Young Writers' Conference

held at _____

on _____

and is entitled to receive this certificate from Colorado Council
International Reading Association and Rocky Mountain Chapter,
Society of Children's Book Writers.

_____
President, CCIRA

_____
President, Local Council CCIRA

_____
President, RMC, SCBW

Figure 3. A Young Writers' Conference Certificate of Participation

X.   Options

1.   Following the conferences many schools display their students' books in the school library. Some schools make these books part of the library collections for as long as their authors attend the school. (It is advisable for students to make at least one additional copy of their books.)

     If the books are to remain in the library for any length of time a card catalog for them can be set up. Students make their own author, title, and subject cards and learn how to file them correctly.

2.   Although the conferences described here are planned for elementary schools, they can include junior and senior high schools as well. In fact, some grade school students, moving up to junior high school, have requested that their new school become involved in the writing projects.

3.   Conference organizers may or may not choose to have the students' books criticized. As a rule, senior high school students, because of their maturity and experience, are more objective critics than junior high students. Some conferences have had students in college writing classes act as critics for the senior high school writers.

4.   Writing books leads naturally to binding books. Finished books range all the way from notebook paper stapled into poster paper covers to stitched books with cloth-covered cardboard covers and decorative endpapers. Many schools set up book-binding workshops in conjunction with writing workshops.

5.   Decisions about selling books at the conference should be made before inviting authors. If it is decided that they may bring books to sell, they will need weeks or months to get those books from their publishers. (Professional writers rarely have stacks of their own books ready to sell — much less to hand out gratis.) It may be more practical to have a local book store provide a booth and handle the sale of books.

6.   One very successful conference that regularly has hundreds of student-writers and several times that many visitors to their Saturday morning meeting has found that printed T-shirts and scarves are fast-selling and expense-defraying items.

READ A BOOK—

WRITE A BOOK

IS YOUR SCHOOL TAKING PART

IN THE

YOUNG WRITERS' CONFERENCE?

FOR DETAILS
ASK YOUR

LOCAL

COUNCIL PRESIDENT

SPONSORED BY

the Colorado Council International Reading Association
and the
Rocky Mountain Chapter – Society of Children's Book Writers

Figure 4. Poster for Promoting Young Writers' Conference

With thanks and appreciation
to
Muriel Brainard

*Vivian Dubrovin and The Longmont,
Colorado Writers Workshop*

Elizabeth J. Hammond

Lee Holland

Merrillyn Kloefkorn

Jeff Oliver

Noel Pazour

Dan Seger

Pat Smedra Jones

who have successfully carried out
our workshops and conferences and their own
with devotion, enthusiasm, and inspiration.

Appendix B

Recommended Reading

REFERENCE, TECHNIQUE, STYLE

Appelbaum, Judith, and Nancy Evans. *How to Get Happily Published.* New York: Harper & Row, 1978.

Bernstein, Theodore M. *The Careful Writer.* New York: Atheneum, 1965.

Flesch, Rudolph. *How to Write, Speak, and Think More Effectively.* New York: Harper & Row, 1960.

Gunning, Robert. *The Technique of Clear Writing.* New York: McGraw-Hill, 1968.

Morris, William, and Mary Morris, eds. *Harper Dictionary of Contemporary Usage.* New York: Harper & Row, 1975.

Strunk, William, Jr., and E. B. White. *The Elements of Style.* New York: Macmillan, 1972.

WRITING FICTION

Brace, Gerald Warner. *The Stuff of Fiction.* New York: Norton, 1969.

Curry, Peggy Simson. *Creating Fiction from Experience.* Boston: The Writer, Inc., 1964.

Gardner, John. *The Art of Fiction.* (Notes on Craft for Young Writers.) New York: Alfred A. Knopf, 1984.

Meredith, Robert C., and John D. Fitzgerald. *Structuring Your Novel.* New York: Barnes & Noble, 1972.

Peck, Robert Newton. *Fiction Is Folks.* (How to Create Unforgettable Characters.) Cincinnati, Ohio: Writer's Digest, 1983.

Raffelock, David. *Writing for the Markets.* New York: Funk & Wagnalls, 1969. (Includes nonfiction.)

Rockwell, F. A. *How to Write Plots That Sell.* New York: Henry Regnery Co., 1975.

————. *Modern Fiction Techniques.* Boston: The Writer, Inc., 1962.

WRITING NONFICTION

Gunther, Max. *Writing the Modern Magazine Article.* Boston: The Writer, Inc., 1968.

Holmes, Marjorie. *Writing the Creative Article.* Boston: The Writer, Inc., 1969.

Rockwell, F. A. *How to Write Nonfiction That Sells.* New York: Henry Regnery Co., 1975.

WRITING FOR CHILDREN

Aiken, Joan. *The Way to Write for Children.* New York: St. Martin's Press, 1982.

Cameron, Eleanor. *The Green and Burning Tree.* New York: Little, Brown, 1969.

Colby, Eleanor. *Writing, Illustrating, and Editing Children's Books.* New York: Hastings House, 1967.

Fitz-Randolph, Jane. *Writing for the Juvenile and Teenage Market.* New York: Barnes & Noble, 1980.

Hunter, Mollie. *Talent Is Not Enough.* New York: Harper & Row, 1975.

Lewis, Claudia. *Writing for Children.* New York: Simon & Schuster, 1954.

Roberts, Ellen E. *The Children's Picture Book.* (How to Write It. How to Sell It.) Cincinnati, Ohio: Writer's Digest Books, 1981.

Southall, Ivan. *A Journey of Discovery: On Writing for Children.* New York: Macmillan, 1976.

Whitney, Phyllis. *Writing Juvenile Fiction.* Boston: The Writer, Inc., 1976.

Yolen, Jane. *Writing Books for Children.* Boston: The Writer, Inc., 1976.

WRITING WITH CHILDREN

Applegate, Mauree. *Freeing Children to Write.* New York: Harper & Row, 1963.

Chenfield, Mimi Brodsky. *Teaching Language Arts Creatively.* New York: Harcourt Brace Jovanovich, Inc., 1978.

Cramer, Ronald L. *Writing, Reading, and Language Growth.* (An Introduction to Language Arts.) New York: Charles E. Merrill Publishing Co., 1978.

Hennings, Dorothy Grant, and Barbara M. Grant. *Content and Craft—Written Expression in the Elementary School.* New York: Prentice-Hall, 1973.

Norton, James H., and Francis Gretton. *Writing Incredibly Short Plays, Poems, Stories.* New York: Harcourt Brace Jovanovich, Inc., 1972.

CHILDREN WRITING

Cassedy, Sylvia. *In Your Own Words.* (A Beginner's Guide to Writing.) New York: Doubleday & Co., 1979.

Dubrovin, Vivian. *Write Your Own Story.* New York: Franklin Watts, 1984.

Jackson, Jacqueline. *Turn Not Pale, Beloved Snail.* New York: Little, Brown, & Co., 1974.

Tchudi, Stephen, and Susan Tchudi. *The Young Writer's Handbook.* New York: Charles Scribner's Sons, 1984.

Yates, Elizabeth. *Someday You'll Write.* New York: Dutton, 1962.

CREATIVITY, IDEAS, AND INSPIRATION

Ashton-Warner, Sylvia. *Teacher.* New York: Simon & Schuster, 1971.

Crawford, Robert P. *The Technique of Creative Thinking.* New York: Hawthorn, 1954.

Koch, Kenneth. *Wishes, Lies, and Dreams.* New York: Chelsea House, 1970.

Livingston, Myra Cohn. *When You Are Alone/It Keeps You Capone.* (An Approach to Creative Writing for Children.) New York: Atheneum, 1973.

Lopate, Phillip. *Being with Children.* New York: Doubleday, 1973.

May, Rollo. *The Courage to Create.* New York: W. W. Norton & Co., 1975.

Mearns, Hughes. *Creative Power.* Mineola, N.Y.: Dover Publishing Company, 1958.

_____. *Creative Youth.* New York: Doubleday, Page & Co., 1927.

Raskin, Bruce. *The Whole Learning Catalogue.* New York: Education Today, 1976.

Rico, Gabriele Lusser. *Writing the Natural Way.* Los Angeles: J. P. Tarcher, Inc. (Distributed by Houghton Mifflin Co.), 1983.

Stewig, John Warren. *Read to Write.* New York: Hawthorne Books, 1975.

von Oech, Roger. *A Whack on the Side of the Head.* (How to Unlock Your Mind for Innovation.) New York: Warner Books, Inc., 1981.

Yolen, Jane. *Touch Magic.* (Fantasy, Faerie and Folklore in the Literature of Childhood.) New York: Philomel Books, 1981.

Zavatsky, Bill, and Ron Padgett, eds. *The Whole Word Catalogue 2.* New York: McGraw-Hill Paperbacks, 1977.

POETRY AND JOURNAL

Ranier, Tristine. *The New Diary*. Los Angeles: J. P. Tarcher, Inc., 1978.

Trefethen, Florence. *Writing a Poem*. Boston: The Writer, Inc., 1970.

Wood, Clement, ed. *The Complete Rhyming Dictionary*. New York: Doubleday, 1936.

Index